THE EASY CLASSIC ROCK

Melody, Lyrics and Simplified Chords

M000165134

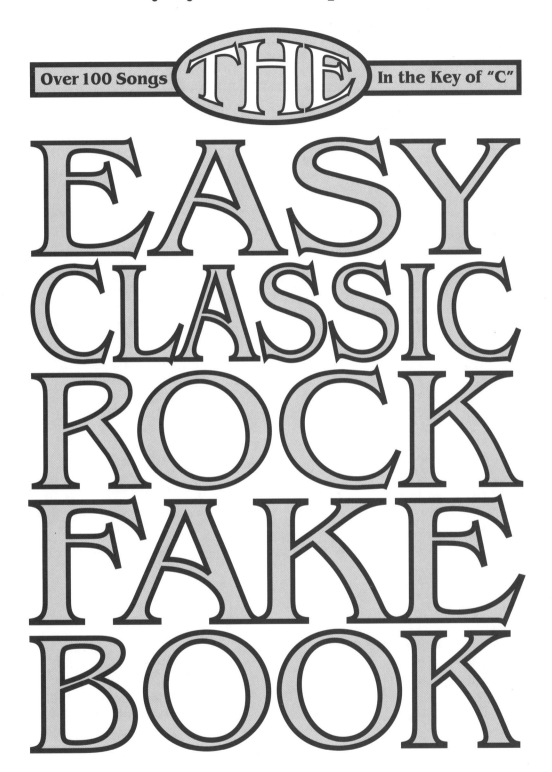

Over 100 Songs THE In the Key of "C"

EASY CLASSIC ROCK FAKE BOOK

ISBN 978-1-4584-0550-0

HAL•LEONARD®
CORPORATION

7777 W. BLUEMOUND RD. P.O. BOX 13819 MILWAUKEE, WI 53213

Visit Hal Leonard Online at
www.halleonard.com

THE EASY CLASSIC ROCK FAKE BOOK

CONTENTS

INTRODUCTION

What Is a Fake Book?

A fake book has one-line music notation consisting of melody, lyrics and chord symbols. This lead sheet format is a "musical shorthand" which is an invaluable resource for all musicians—hobbyists to professionals.

Here's how *The Easy Classic Rock Fake Book* differs from most standard fake books:

- All songs are in the key of C.

- Only five basic chord types are used—major, minor, seventh, diminished and augmented.

- The music notation is larger for ease of reading.

In the event that you haven't used chord symbols to create accompaniment, or your experience is limited, a chord speller chart is included at the back of the book to help you get started.

Have fun!

AMERICAN GIRL

Words and Music by
TOM PETTY

Moderately fast Rock

Well, she was an A - mer - i - can
Well, it was kind - a cold that ___ night. ___

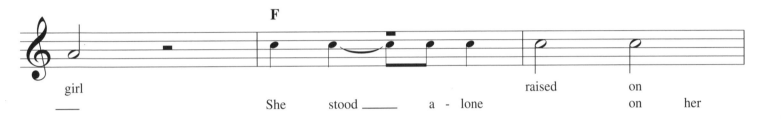

girl
___   She stood ___ a - lone   raised on
                                              on her

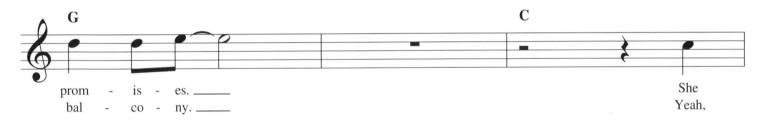

prom - is - es. ___   She
bal - co - ny. ___   Yeah,

could - n't help   think - in' ___ that there was a
she could hear the   cars roll ___ by ___ out on

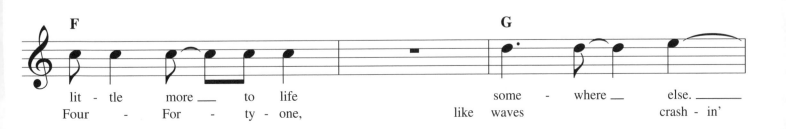

lit - tle more ___ to life   some - where ___ else. ___
Four - For - ty - one,   like waves   crash - in'

6

in on the beach. _   Af - ter all, it was a

C   **F**

great big _____ world _____   with lots of

mo - ment ___ there _____   he crept _

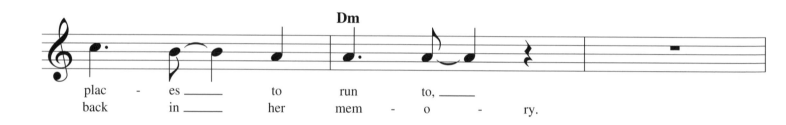

Dm

plac - es _____ to run to, _____

back in _____ her mem - o - ry.

G

and if _____ she had to die   try -

God, it's _____ so pain - ful when some - thing _ that's

- in', she _____   had one lit - tle prom - ise

so close ___   is still so

she was gon - na keep. _____
far out of reach. _____

Oh yeah, all right, take it

eas - y, ba - by, make it last all night.

She was an A -

mer - i - can girl. _____ *(Instrumental)*

1

2

AGAINST THE WIND

Words and Music by
BOB SEGER

Medium Rock beat

It seems like yes - ter - day,   but it was long a -
And the years rolled slow - ly past.   And I found my - self a -
Instrumental

go. _____   Ja - ney was love - ly. She was the   queen of my nights,
lone, _____   sur - round-ed by stran - gers I   thought were my friends.

there in the dark - ness with the   ra - di - o   play - in' low, ___ and
I found my - self ____ fur - ther and   fur - ther from   my ___ home, __ and

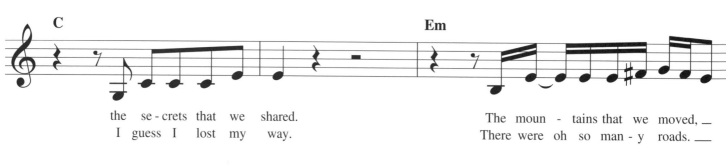

the se - crets that we shared.   The moun - tains that we moved, _
I guess I lost my way.   There were oh so man - y roads. __

I was   caught like a wild fire out of con - trol _____   till there was
liv - in' to run and run - nin' to   live. _____   Nev - er

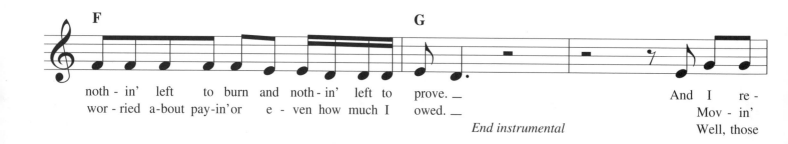

noth - in' left to burn and noth - in' left to prove. _   And I re -
wor - ried a-bout pay-in' or e - ven how much I owed. _   Mov - in'
End instrumental   Well, those

ALL RIGHT NOW

Words and Music by ANDY FRASER
and PAUL RODGERS

Moderately, with a strong beat

There she stood in the street _____
home to my place, _____

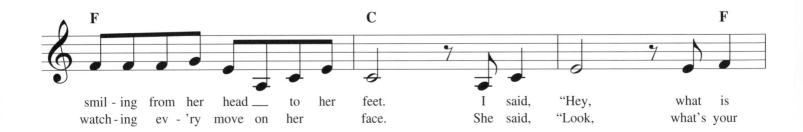

smil-ing from her head _____ to her feet. I said, "Hey, what is
watch-ing ev-'ry move on her face. She said, "Look, what's your

this?" _____ Now, ba-by, may-be may-be she's in need _____ of a
game, _____ ba-by? Are you tryin' to put me in

kiss. I said, "Hey, what's your name, ba-by?
shame?" I said, "Slow, don't go so fast.

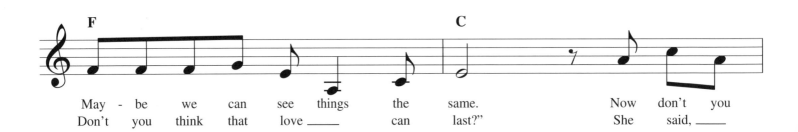

May-be we can see things the same. Now don't you
Don't you think that love _____ can last?" She said, _____

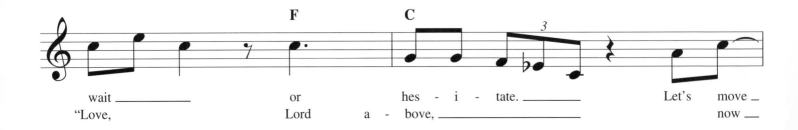

wait _____ or hes-i-tate. _____ Let's move _____
"Love, Lord a-bove, _____ now _____

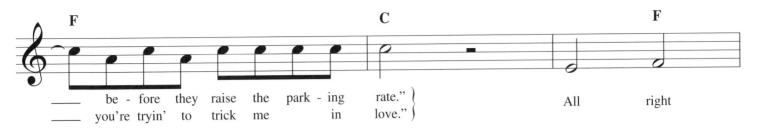

be - fore they raise the park - ing rate."
you're tryin' to trick me in love." All right

now, _____ ba - by, it's all _____ right _____ now.

All right now, _____ ba - by, it's all _____ right _____

now. I took her now.

All right now, _____ ba - by, it's all _____

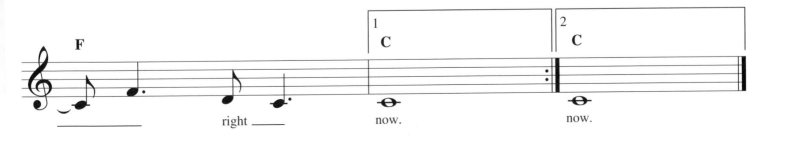

_____ right _____ now. now.

ANOTHER ONE BITES THE DUST

Words and Music by
JOHN DEACON

Steady Rock

(Instrumental)

(3.) There are

(1.) Steve walks war-i-ly down __ the street with the brim pulled way down low.
(2.) How do you think I'm going to get a-long with-out you, when you're gone? You
plen-ty of ways you can hurt __ a man and bring him to the ground. You can

Ain't no sound but the sound of his feet; __ ma-chine guns read-y to go. __ Are you
took me for ev-'ry-thing that I had __ and kicked me out on my own. __ Are you
beat him, you can cheat him, you can treat him bad __ and leave him when he's down. _ But I'm

read-y, hey! __ Are you read-y for this? __ Are you hang-ing on the edge of your seat? _
hap-py? _____ Are you sat-is-fied? __ How long can you stand the heat? _
read-y, _____ yes, I'm read-y for you. __ I'm stand-ing on my own two feet. __

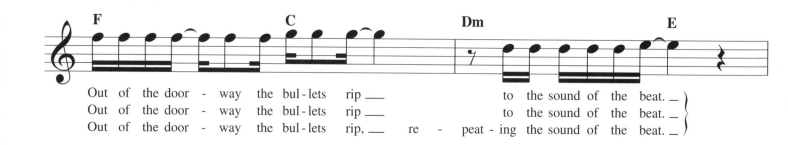

Out of the door-way the bul-lets rip __ to the sound of the beat. _ ⎫
Out of the door-way the bul-lets rip __ to the sound of the beat. _ ⎬
Out of the door-way the bul-lets rip, __ re-peat-ing the sound of the beat. _ ⎭

An-oth-er one bites the dust. _

An-

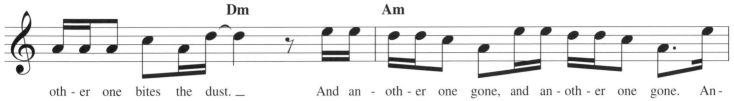

oth - er one bites the dust. __ And an - oth - er one gone, and an - oth - er one gone. An -

oth - er one bites the dust. ___ Hey! ___ I'm gon - na get you, too. An -

oth - er one bites the dust. __ oth - er one bites the dust. __ An -

oth - er one bites the dust, __ an - oth - er one bites the dust. __ An -

oth - er one bites the dust, __ an - oth - er one bites the dust. __

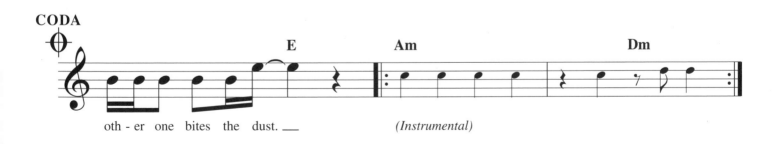

oth - er one bites the dust. __ (Instrumental)

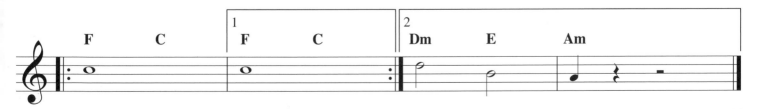

AUTHORITY SONG

Words and Music by
JOHN MELLENCAMP

Moderately fast Rock

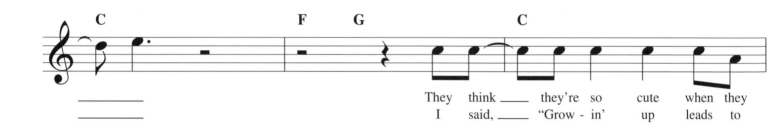

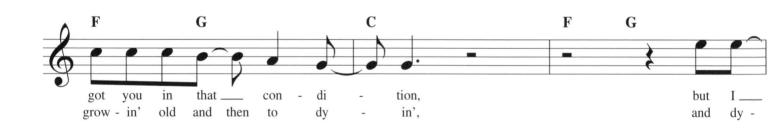

Well, I _____ fight au - thor - i - ty. Au -

thor - i - ty al - ways wins. _____ Well, I been

do - in' it since __ I was a young kid, and I've come out grin - nin'.

Well, I _____ fight au - thor - i - ty. Au - thor - i - ty al - ways wins. __

_____ (Instrumental)

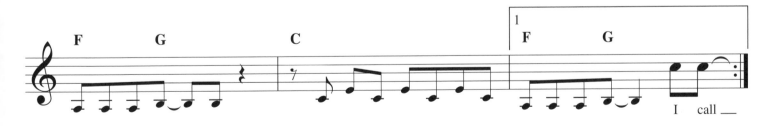

I call __

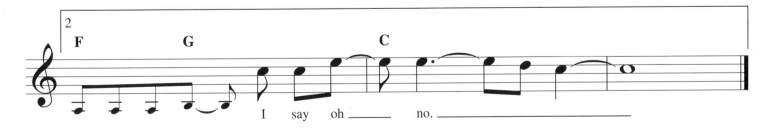

I say oh _____ no. _____

BABE, I'M GONNA LEAVE YOU

Words and Music by ANNE BREDON,
JIMMY PAGE and ROBERT PLANT

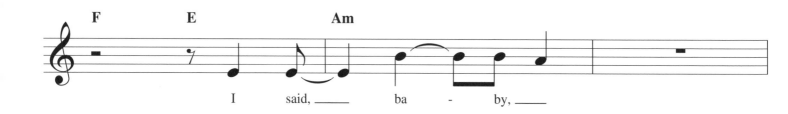

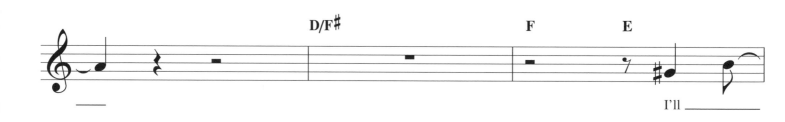

leave you when the _____ sum - mer comes a - roll - in',

leave ___ you when ___ the sum - mer ___ comes ___

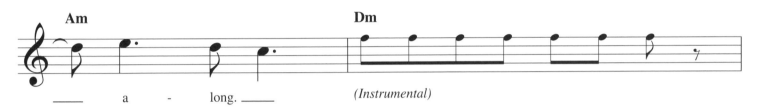

___ a - long. ____ *(Instrumental)*

Babe, babe, ___ babe, ____ babe, ___ babe, ____ babe, ___ ba -

- by, mm, ba - by, I _____ wan - na leave _____ you. ____

I ain't jok - in', ____ wom - an, I've got to ____

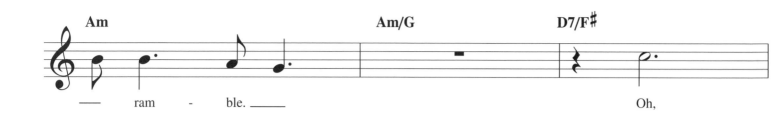

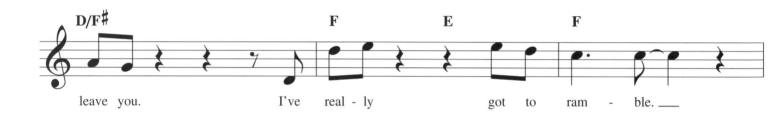

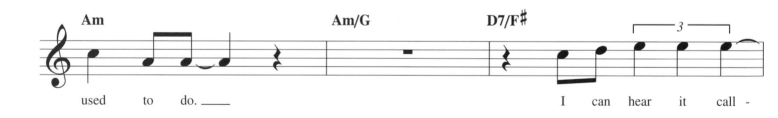

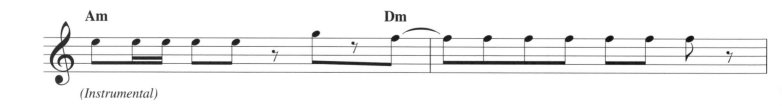

AQUALUNG

Music by IAN ANDERSON
Lyrics by JENNIE ANDERSON

Moderately

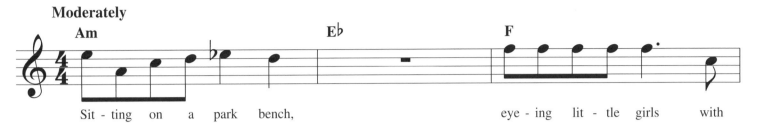

Sit - ting on a park bench, eye - ing lit - tle girls with

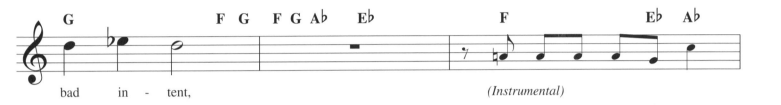

bad in - tent, (Instrumental)

snot is run - ning down his nose,

greas - y fin - gers smear - ing shab - by clothes. _____

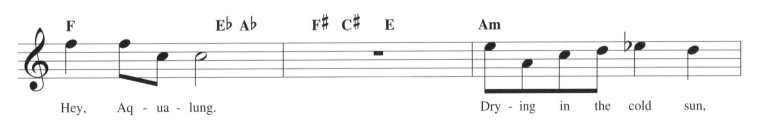

Hey, Aq - ua - lung. Dry - ing in the cold sun,

watch - ing as the frill - y pant - ies run.

22

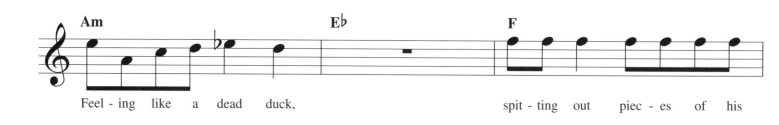

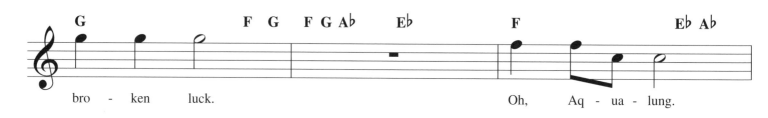

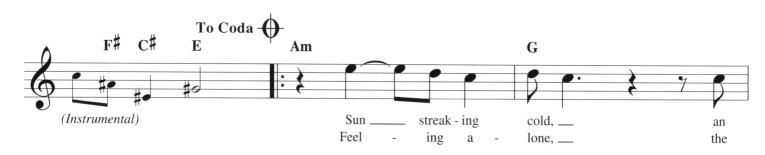

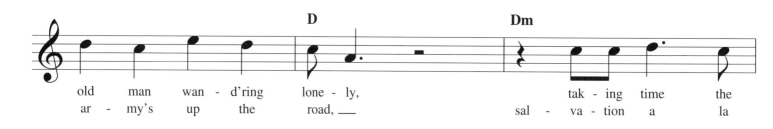

goes down to the bog __ and warms his feet.
poor old sod, you see __ it's on - ly me.

Faster

Do you still re - mem - ber De - cem - ber's fog - gy

freeze when the ice that clings on - to your beard was

scream - ing ag - o - ny? And you snatch your rat - tling

last breaths with deep - sea div - er sounds and the

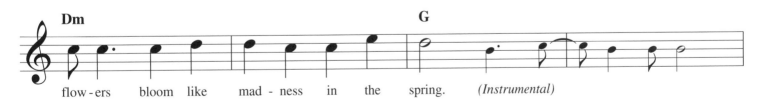

flow - ers bloom like mad - ness in the spring. *(Instrumental)*

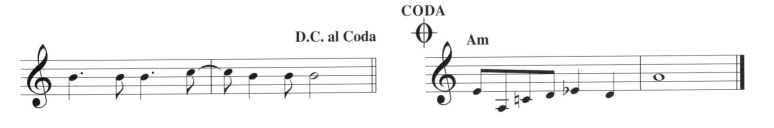

BABY, I LOVE YOUR WAY

Words and Music by
PETER FRAMPTON

Moderately

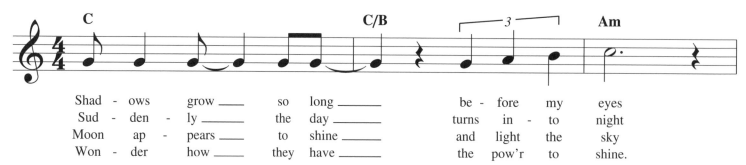

Shad - ows grow ___ so long ___ be - fore my eyes
Sud - den - ly ___ the day ___ turns in - to night
Moon ap - pears ___ to shine ___ and light the sky
Won - der how ___ they have ___ the pow'r to shine.

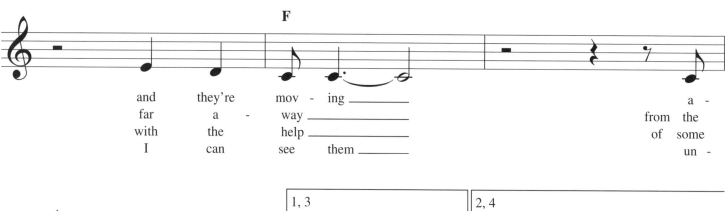

and they're mov - ing ___ a
far a - way ___ from the
with the help ___ of some
I can see them ___ un -

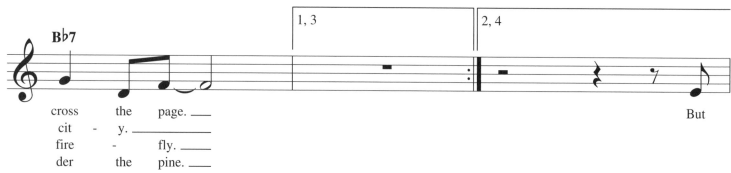

cross the page. ___ But
cit - y. ___
fire - fly. ___
der the pine. ___

don't hes - i - tate ___

'cause your love ___ won't

I wish I could buy one

out of sea - son.

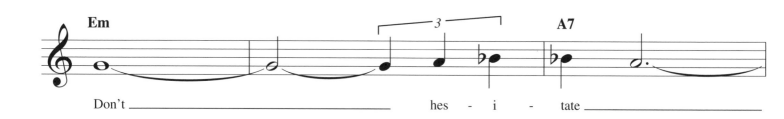

Don't _____ hes - i - tate _____

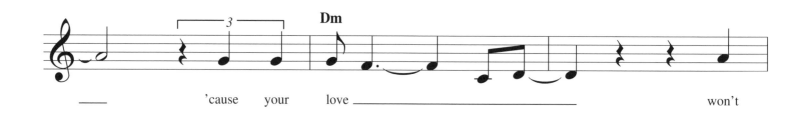

____ 'cause your love _____ won't

wait. _____   Ooh,
Wan - na
Wan - na

ba - by, I love ___ your way. _____
tell you I love ___ your way. _____
be with you night ___ and day. _____

BEST OF MY LOVE

Words and Music by JOHN DAVID SOUTHER,
DON HENLEY and GLENN FREY

28

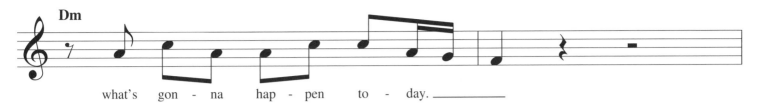

what's gon - na hap - pen to - day. _____

You see it your ___ way and I see it mine, ___ but we

both see it slip - pin' a - way. _____ You know we al - ways had each

oth - er, ba - by, I guess that was - n't e - nough; _____

oh, _____ but here in my heart ___ I give you the best ___ of my ___

love. Oh, _____ sweet dar - lin',

you get the best of my love. ___ Oh, _____ love.

BADGE

Words and Music by ERIC CLAPTON
and GEORGE HARRISON

Moderately

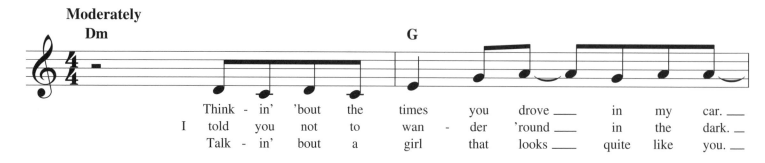

Think - in' 'bout the times you drove ___ in my car. ___
I told you not to wan - der 'round ___ in the dark. ___
Talk - in' 'bout a girl that looks ___ quite like you. ___

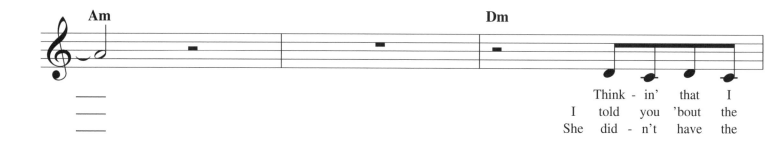

___ Think - in' that I
___ I told you 'bout the
___ She did - n't have the

might have drove ___ you too far. _____
swans, that they live in the park. ___
time to wait ___ in the queue. ___

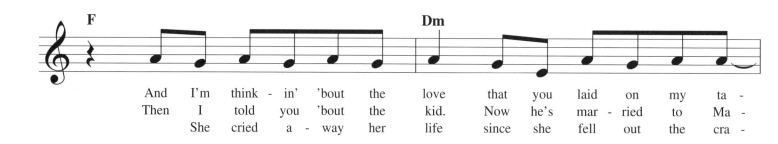

And I'm think - in' 'bout the love that you laid on my ta -
Then I told you 'bout the kid. Now he's mar - ried to Ma -
She cried a - way her life since she fell out the cra -

To Coda ⊕

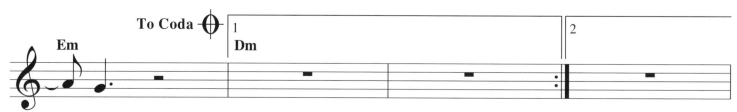

- ble.
- bel.
- dle.

Yes, I told _____ you that the life goes up and down. _ Don't you no-

-tice how the wheel goes 'round. And you'd bet - ter pick your-self up

from the ground _ be-fore _____ they bring the cur - tain down, ___ yes, be-fore _

_____ they bring the cur - tain down. ___ Ooh. _____

Get up, get up, get up.

Yeah _____ yeah yeah. ___

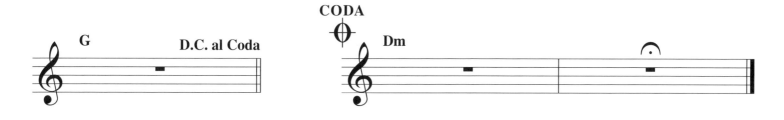

BARRACUDA

Words and Music by NANCY WILSON, ANN WILSON,
MICHAEL DEROSIER and ROGER FISHER

Moderately fast

So this ain't the end, ___ I saw you a-gain ___ to-

day. I had to turn my heart a-way. ___

Smile like the sun, ___ kiss-es for ev - 'ry-

one, and tales ___ it ___ nev-er fails. ___

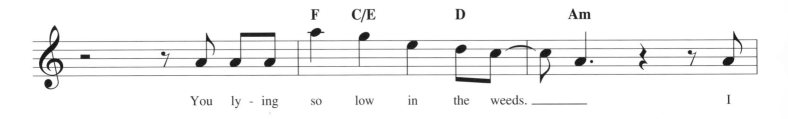

You ly-ing so low in the weeds. ___ I

bet you gon-na am-bush me. ___ You'd have me

down, down, ___ down, ___ down on my ___ knees ___ now

real thing don't do the trick, ___ you bet - ter

make up some - thing quick. _____ You gon - na burn, burn, __ burn, __

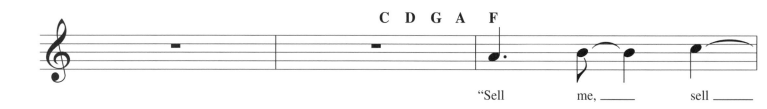

__ burn, burn to the wick. _____

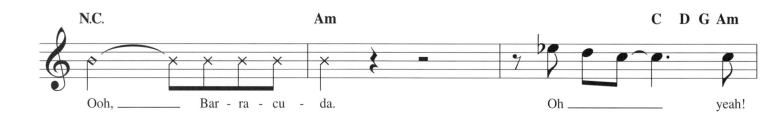

Ooh, _____ Bar - ra - cu - da. Oh _____ yeah!

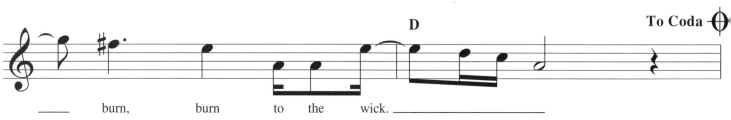

"Sell me, _____ sell _____

___ you," the por - poise said. Dive down, ___ deep _____

___ to save my head. You, _____

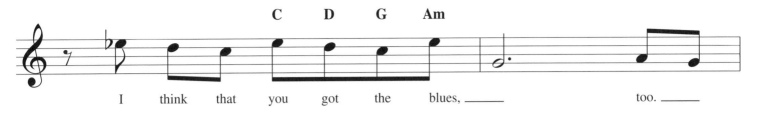

I think that you got the blues, _____ too. _____

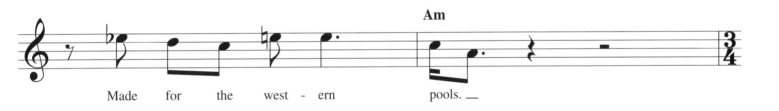

All that _____ night _____

_____ and all the next swam with-out look-ing back.

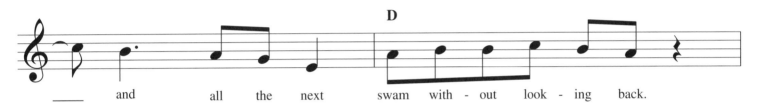

Made for the west-ern pools. _____

D.S. al Coda

Sil - ly, sil - ly fools. _____ The

CODA

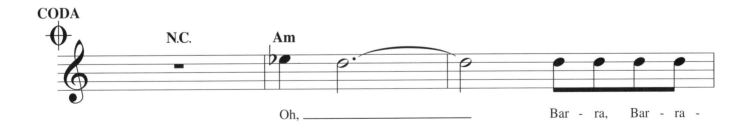

Oh, _____ Bar - ra, Bar - ra -

cu - da. _____ Yeah!

BORN TO BE WILD

Words and Music by
MARS BONFIRE

Moderate Rock beat

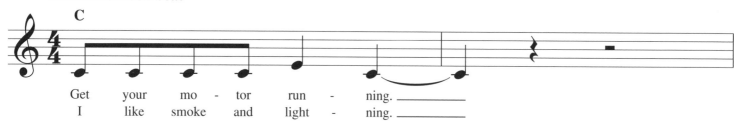

Get your mo - tor run - ning. _____
I like smoke and light - ning. _____

Head out on the high - way _____   look - ing for ad - ven - ture
Heav - y met - al thun - der _____   rac - ing in the wind

in what - ev - er comes our way. _____
and the feel - ing that I'm un - der. _____

Yeah, dar - ling, gon - na make it hap - pen,

take the world in a love em - brace. _   Fire _ all of your guns _

THE BOYS ARE BACK IN TOWN

Words and Music by
PHILIP PARRIS LYNOTT

Moderately bright

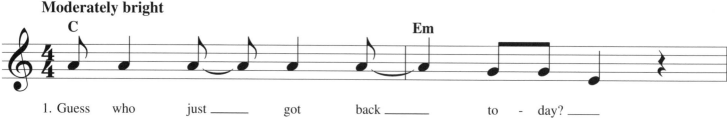

1. Guess who just ____ got back ____ to - day? ____
2., 3. (*See additional lyrics*)

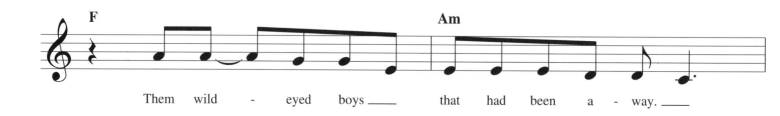

Them wild - eyed boys ____ that had been a - way. ____

Had - n't changed, had - n't much to say, but, man, I still think them ____

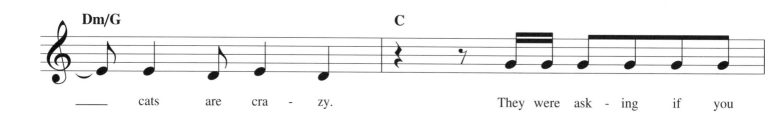

____ cats are cra - zy. They were ask - ing if you

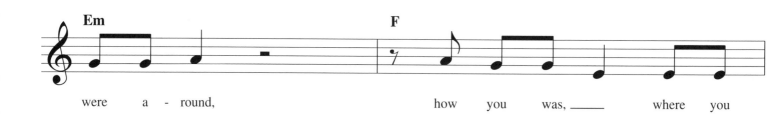

were a - round, how you was, ____ where you

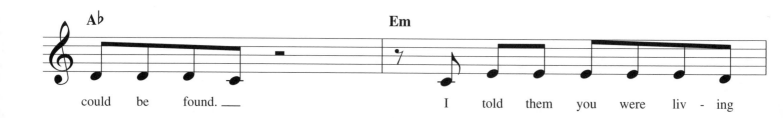

could be found. ____ I told them you were liv - ing

down - town,   driv - ing all the old men cra - zy.   The

Chorus

boys   are back   in town,   the   boys   are back   in town.

I   say, the   boys   are back   in   town, _____   the

boys   are back   in town.   The   boys   are back   in town, the

boys   are back in town,   the   boys   are back in town,   the   boys   are back   in town.

(*Instrumental*)

Interlude

Spread the word a-round; guess __ who's back in

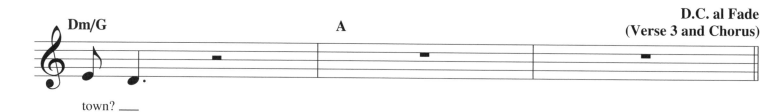

town? __

Additional Lyrics

2. You know that chick that used to dance a lot
   Every night she'd be on the floor shaking what she'd got
   Man, when I tell you she was cool, she was hot
   I mean she was steaming.

   And that time over at Johnny's place
   Well, this chick got up and she slapped Johnny's face
   Man, we just fell about the place
   If that chick don't wanna know, forget her.
   (Chorus & Interlude)

3. Friday night they'll be dressed to kill
   Down at Dino's Bar and Grill
   The drink will flow and blood will spill
   And if the boys want to fight, you better let 'em.

   That jukebox in the corner blasting out my favorite song
   The nights are getting warmer, it won't be long
   It won't be long till summer comes
   Now that the boys are here again.
   (Chorus and Fade)

BURNING FOR YOU

Words and Music by DONALD ROESER
and RICHARD MELTZER

Moderate Rock

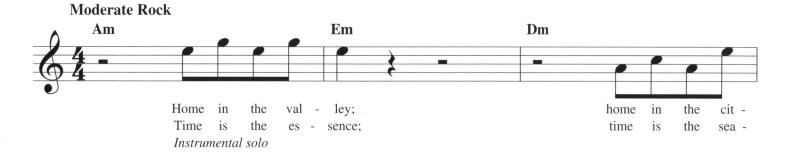

Home in the val - ley;   home in the cit -
Time is the es - sence;   time is the sea -
Instrumental solo

y.   Home is - n't pret - ty;
son.   Time ain't no rea - son;

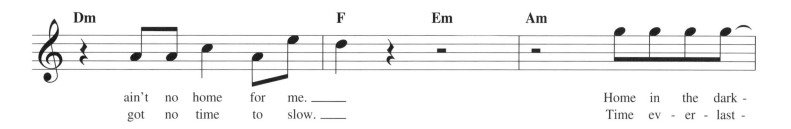

ain't no home   for me. _____   Home in the dark -
got no time   to slow. _____   Time ev - er - last -

- ness;   home on the high - way.
- ing;   time to play "B" _____ sides.

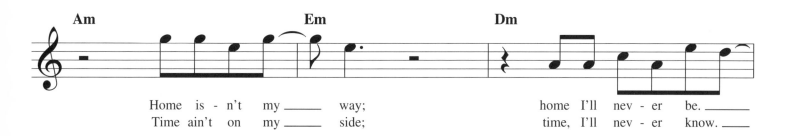

Home is - n't my _____ way;   home I'll nev - er be. _____
Time ain't on my _____ side;   time, I'll nev - er know. _____

42

Solo ends

Burn out the day; _____

burn out the night. ____

{ (1.,3.) I can't see no
{ (2.) I'm not the one to

rea - son to put up a fight. _____
tell you what's wrong or what's right. _____

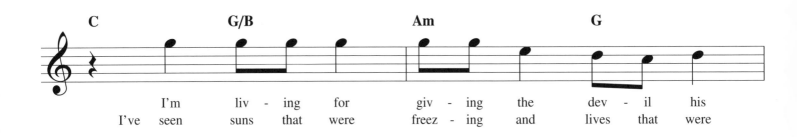

I'm liv - ing for giv - ing the dev - il his
I've seen suns that were freez - ing and lives that were

To Coda ⊕

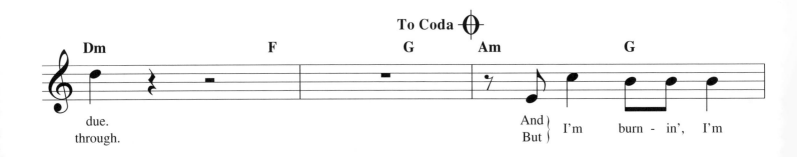

due.
through.

And }
But } I'm burn - in', I'm

burn - in', I'm burn - in' for you. _____

I'm burn - in', I'm burn - in', I'm burn - in' for you. _____

_____ (Instrumental)   1.   2. D.C. al Coda

CODA

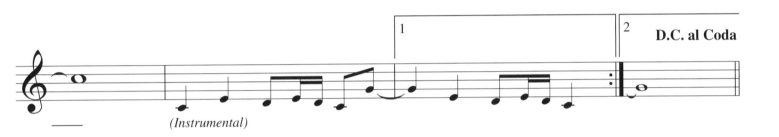

And I'm burn - in', I'm burn - in', I'm burn - in' for you. _____

I'm burn - in', I'm burn - in', I'm burn - in' for you. __

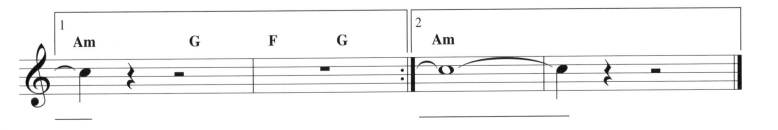

burn - in' ___

BREAKDOWN

Words and Music by
TOM PETTY

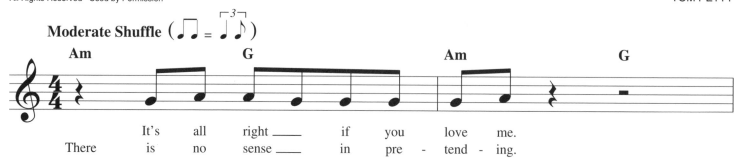

It's all right ____ if you love me.
There is no sense ____ in pre - tend - ing.

It's all right ____ if you don't. ____
Your eyes give ____ you a - way. ____

I'm not a - fraid of you run - ning a - way, hon - ey.
Some - thing in - side you is feel - ing like I do. ____

I get the ____ feel - ing you ____ won't. ____
We've said all ____ there is to ____ say. ____

Ba - by, break down.
(D.S.) Break down.

Go a - head, give it to me.

Break down, hon - ey, take _____ me through _ the night. __

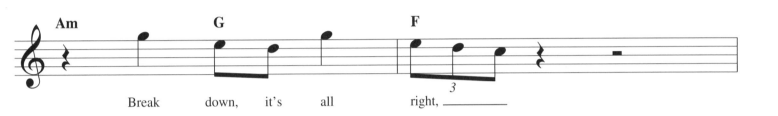

Break down, now I'm stand - in' here, can't you see? ____

Break down, it's all right, _____

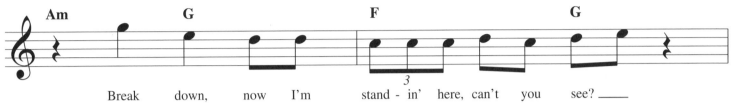

it's all right, it's all

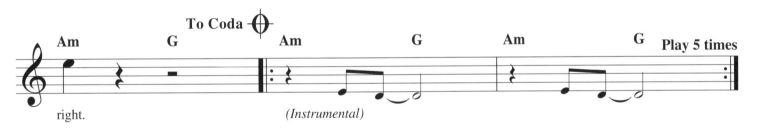

right. (Instrumental)

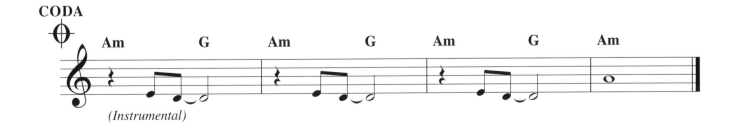

(Instrumental)

BROWN EYED GIRL

Words and Music by
VAN MORRISON

Moderately

1. Hey, where did   we _____ go?   Days __ when the rains __
2., 3. *(See additional lyrics)*

_____ came,   down __ in the hol - low

play - in' a new ____ game,   laugh - ing and a -

run - ning, hey, ___ hey,   skip - ping and a - jump - ing.

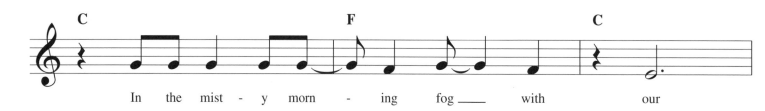

In the mist - y morn - ing fog ____ with   our

hearts a - thump - in', and   you,   my   brown   eyed

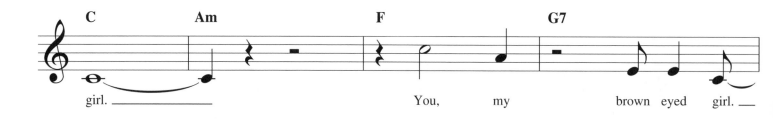

girl. _____   You,   my   brown eyed girl. __

C   G7

Do you re-mem - ber when

Chorus
C   F

we used to sing: ___ sha la ___ la la ___ la la ___ la la ___

C   G7   C

___ la la la te da. ___   Sha la ___ la la ___

F   C   G7

___ la la ___ la la ___ la la la te da ___ la te da. ___

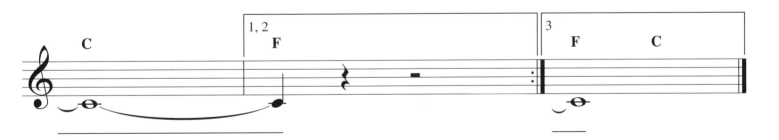

C   1, 2   3
                F   F   C

Additional Lyrics

2. Whatever happened to Tuesday and so slow
Going down the old mine with a transistor radio
Standing in the sunlight laughing
Hiding behind a rainbow's wall
Slipping and a-sliding
All along the waterfall
With you, my brown eyed girl
You, my brown eyed girl.
Do you remember when we used to sing:
Chorus

3. So hard to find my way, now that I'm all on my own
I saw you just the other day, my, how you have grown
Cast my memory back there, Lord
Sometime I'm overcome thinking 'bout
Making love in the green grass
Behind the stadium
With you, my brown eyed girl
With you, my brown eyed girl.
Do you remember when we used to sing:
Chorus

CARRY ON WAYWARD SON

Words and Music by
KERRY LIVGREN

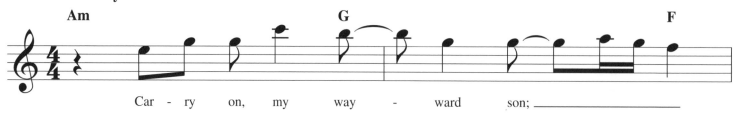

Car - ry on, my way - ward son; _____

there'll be peace when you ____ are done. __ Lay your wea - ry head _

____ to rest; _____ don't you cry no ____ more.

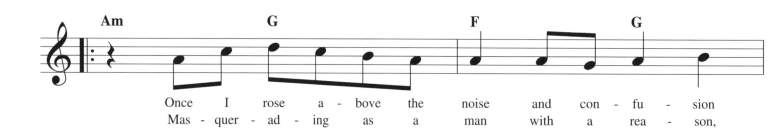

Once I rose a - bove the noise and con - fu - sion
Mas - quer - ad - ing as a man with a rea - son,

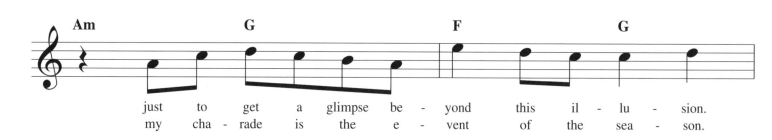

just to get a glimpse be - yond this il - lu - sion.
my cha - rade is the e - vent of the sea - son.

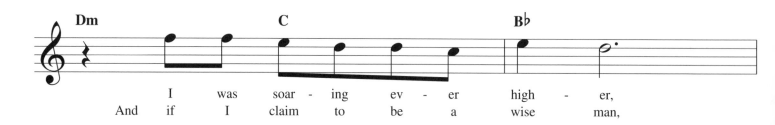

I was soar - ing ev - er high - er,
And if I claim to be a wise man,

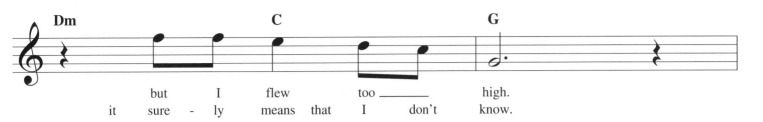

but I flew too _____ high.
it sure - ly means that I don't know.

Though my eyes could see, I still was a blind man.
On a storm - y sea of mov - ing e - mo - tion,

Though my mind could think, I still was a mad - man.
tossed a - bout, I'm like a ship on the o - cean.

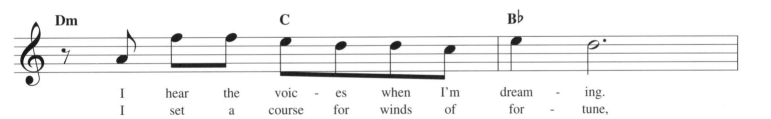

I hear the voic - es when I'm dream - ing.
I set a course for winds of for - tune,

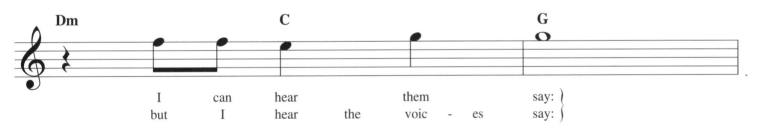

I can hear them say:
but I hear the voic - es say:

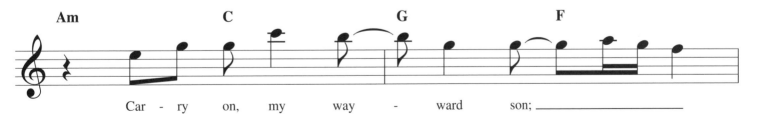

Car - ry on, my way - ward son; _____

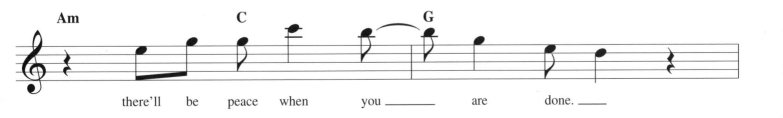

there'll be peace when you _____ are done. _____

50

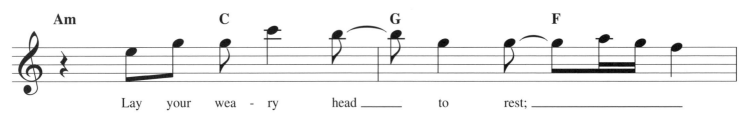

Lay your wea - ry head _____ to rest; _____

don't you cry no _____ more. *(Instrumental)*

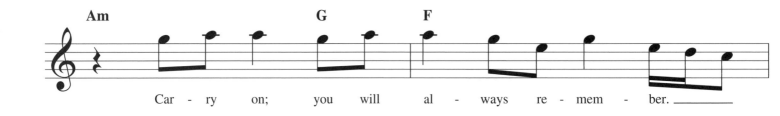

Car - ry on; you will al - ways re - mem - ber. _____

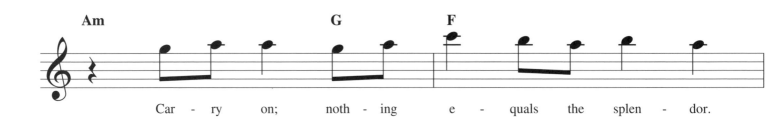

Car - ry on; noth - ing e - quals the splen - dor.

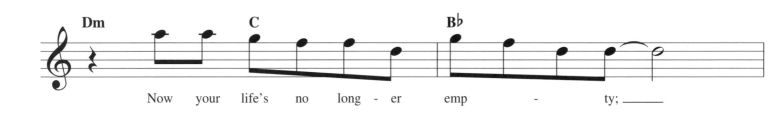

Now your life's no long - er emp - ty; _____

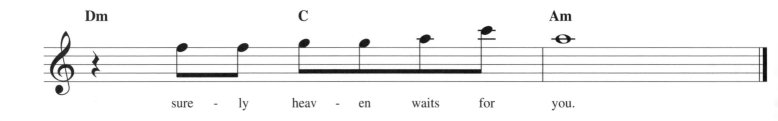

sure - ly heav - en waits for you.

DON'T STOP BELIEVIN'

Words and Music by STEVE PERRY,
NEAL SCHON and JONATHAN CAIN

Moderately fast

Just a small-town girl, ____ livin' in a
Just a cit - y boy, ____ born and raised in

lone - ly world. _____ She took the mid-night train __ go - in'
south De - troit. _____ He took the mid-night train __ go - in'

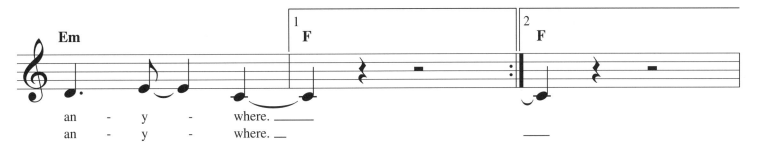

an - y - where. _____
an - y - where. __

A sing - er in a smok - y room. __ The smell of wine and

cheap per - fume. _____ For a smile _ they can share the night. It goes

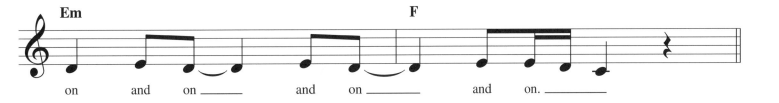

on and on _____ and on _____ and on. _____

52

Am **F** **C**
some were born to sing the blues. _____ Oh, the mov - ie nev -

D.S. al Coda
(with repeat)

G **Em** **F**
- er ends; _ it goes on and on ___ and on _____ and on. _____

CODA

C **G**
Don't ___ stop be - liev - in'.

Am **F** **C**
Hold on to the feel - in', _____ street - light

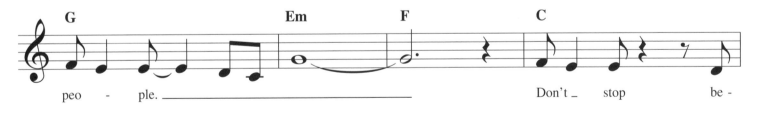

G **Em** **F** **C**
peo - ple. _____ Don't _ stop be -

G **Am** **F**
liev - ing. Hold on, _____

C **G** **C**
street - light peo - ple. _____

COLD AS ICE

Words and Music by MICK JONES
and LOU GRAMM

Brightly, with a beat

You're as cold ____ as ice. ____ You're will - ing to

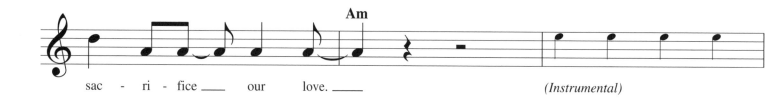

sac - ri - fice ____ our love. ____ (Instrumental)

You nev - er
You want

take ad - vice. ____ }
par - a - dise. ____ }
Some - day you'll ____ pay the price, I

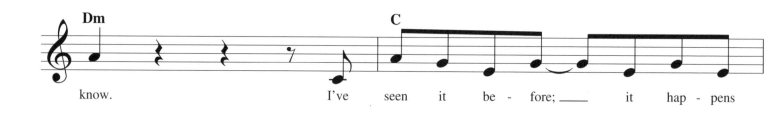

know. I've seen it be - fore; ____ it hap - pens

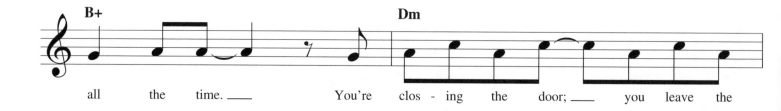

all the time. ____ You're clos - ing the door; ____ you leave the

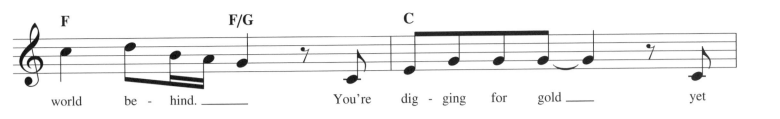

world be - hind. _____ You're dig - ging for gold _____ yet

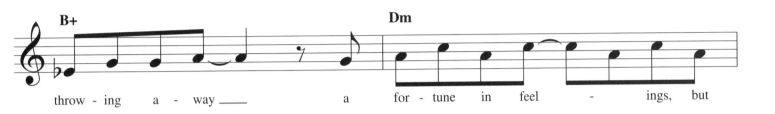

throw - ing a - way _____ a for - tune in feel - ings, but

some-day you'll pay. *(Instrumental)*

some-day you'll pay. Cold as

ice. You know _____ that you are. Cold as

ice. *(Instrumental)*

Ooh. _____

COME SAIL AWAY

Words and Music by
DENNIS DeYOUNG

Moderately slow

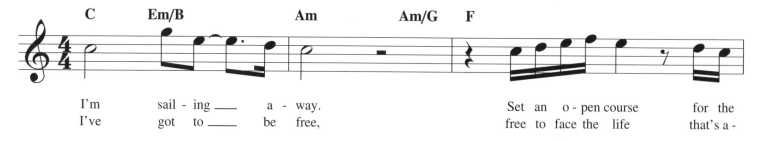

I'm sail - ing ____ a - way.
I've got to ____ be free,
Set an o - pen course for the
free to face the life that's a -

vir - gin sea. 'Cause
head of me. On board I'm the cap - tain, ____

so climb a - board. We'll search for to - mor - row ____

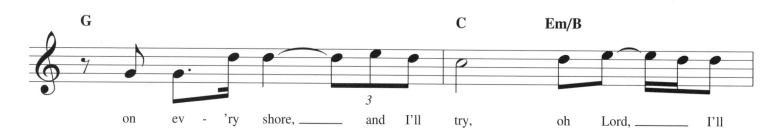

on ev - 'ry shore, ____ and I'll try, oh Lord, ____ I'll

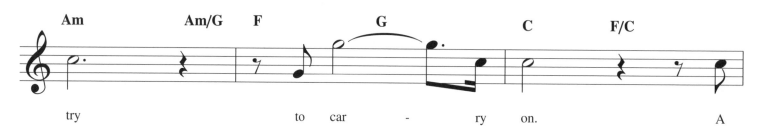

try to car - ry on. A

gath - er - ing ____ of an - gels ____ ap - peared a - bove ____ my ____ head. ____
thought that they ____ were an - gels ____ but much to my ____ sur - prise, ____

They
we

To Coda ⊕

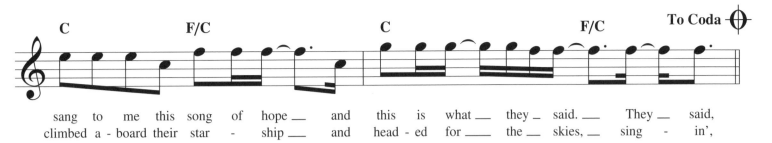

sang to me this song of hope ___ and this is what ___ they ___ said. ___ They ___ said,
climbed a - board their star - ship ___ and head - ed for ___ the ___ skies, ___ sing - in',

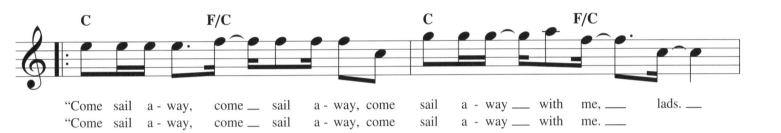

"Come sail a - way, come ___ sail a - way, come sail a - way ___ with me, ___ lads. ___
"Come sail a - way, come ___ sail a - way, come sail a - way ___ with me. ___

1

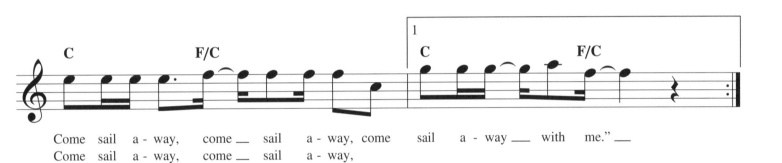

Come sail a - way, come ___ sail a - way, come sail a - way ___ with me." ___
Come sail a - way, come ___ sail a - way,

2

D.S. al Coda

CODA ⊕

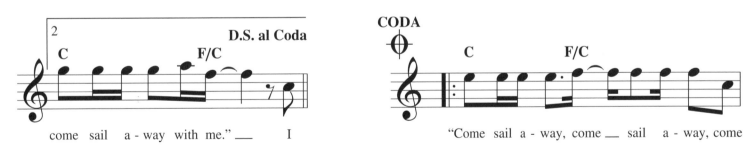

come sail a - way with me." ___ I

"Come sail a - way, come ___ sail a - way, come

1

2

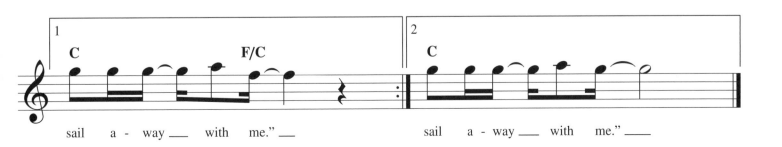

sail a - way ___ with me." ___

sail a - way ___ with me." ___

COME TOGETHER

Words and Music by JOHN LENNON
and PAUL McCARTNEY

Moderately slow

Here come old flat - top, he come groov - ing up slow - ly, He got

Joo Joo eye - ball, he one ho - ly roll - er, he got

hair down to his knee.___ Got to be a jok - er, he just

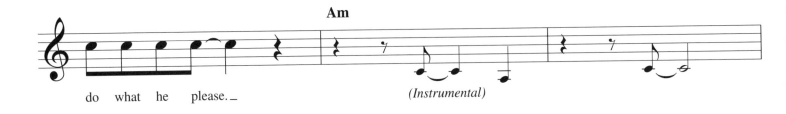

do what he please.___ *(Instrumental)*

He wear no shoe - shine, he got
He bag pro - duc - tion, he got
He roll - er coast - er, he got

toe - jam foot - ball, he got mon - key fin - ger, he shoot
wal - rus gum - boot, he got O - no side - board, he one
ear - ly warn - ing, he got mud - dy wa - ter, he one

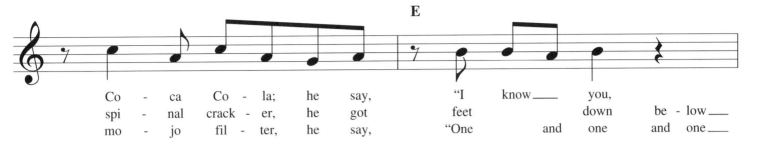

Co - ca Co - la; he say, "I know___ you,
spi - nal crack - er, he got feet down be - low___
mo - jo fil - ter, he say, "One and one and one___

you know me.___ One thing I can tell you is you
___ his knee.___ Hold you in his arm - chair, you can
___ is three." ___ Got to be good - look - ing 'cause he's

got to be free." ___
feel his dis - ease. ___ } Come to - geth - er, ___ right
so hard to see. ___

now, ___ o - ver me. ___

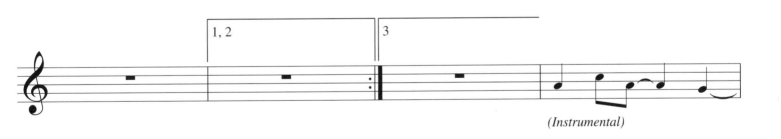

(Instrumental)

Come to - geth - er, ___ yeah!

CRAZY LITTLE THING CALLED LOVE

Words and Music by
FREDDIE MERCURY

Moderately fast Shuffle

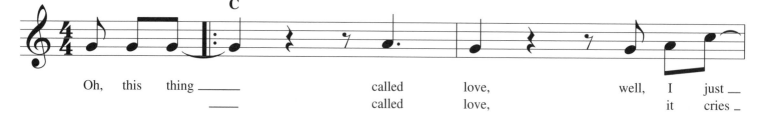

Oh, this thing _____ called love, well, I just _____

_____ called love, it cries _____

_____ can't _____ han - dle it. _____ This thing _____ called

_____ in a cra - dle all night. It swings, _____ it

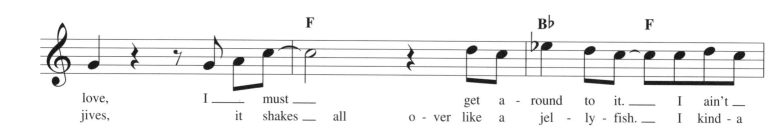

love, I _____ must _____ get a - round to it. _____ I ain't _____

jives, it shakes _____ all o - ver like a jel - ly - fish. _____ I kind - a

read - y. } Cra - zy lit - tle thing called love.
like it. }

1
Well, this thing _____

2
There goes my ba - by; _____

she knows ___ how to rock and roll. ___ She drives ___ me

cra - zy. ___ She gives me hot and cold fe - ver. She

leaves me in a cool, cool sweat. *(Instrumental)*

I got - ta be cool, ___ re - lax, ___

___ a - get hip, ___ a - get on my tracks. Take a

back seat, hitch - hike ___ and take a long ride ___ on a

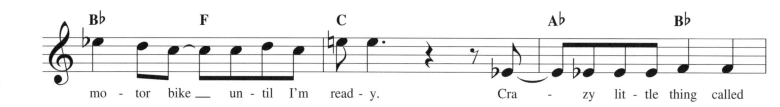

mo - tor bike __ un - til I'm read - y. Cra - zy lit - tle thing called

love. I got - ta be cool, ____ re - lax, __

____ a - get hip, ____ a - get on my tracks. Take a

back seat, ____ hitch - hike ____ to take a lit - tle long ride ____ on my

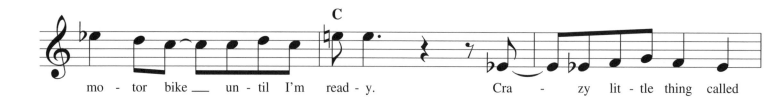

mo - tor bike __ un - til I'm read - y. Cra - zy lit - tle thing called

love. This thing ____ called

love, I _____ just _____ can't ___ han - dle it. _____ This

thing called love, I _____ must _____ get a -

round to it. ___ I ain't ___ read - y. Cra - zy lit - tle thing called

love, cra - zy lit - tle thing called love, cra -

- zy lit - tle thing called love, cra - zy lit - tle thing called

love, hey, cra - zy lit - tle thing called love.

DAY TRIPPER

Words and Music by JOHN LENNON
and PAUL McCARTNEY

Moderate Rock

(*Instrumental*)

Got a good rea - son
She's a big teas - er,
Tried___ to please___ her,

for tak - ing the eas - y way out._____
she took me half___ the way there._____
she on - ly played___ one-night stands._____

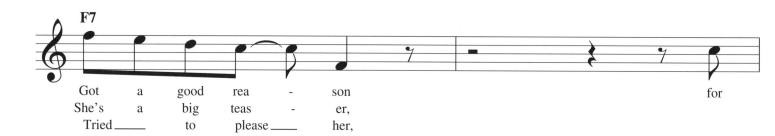

Got a good rea - son   for
She's a big teas - er,
Tried___ to please___ her,

tak - ing the eas - y way out,_____ now.   She was a
she took me half___ the way there,_____ now.   She was a
she on - ly played___ one-night stands,_____ now. She was a

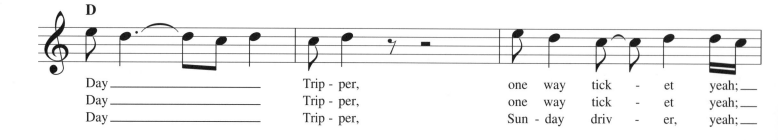

Day_____ Trip - per,   one way tick - et yeah;___
Day_____ Trip - per,   one way tick - et yeah;___
Day_____ Trip - per,   Sun - day driv - er, yeah;___

DO IT AGAIN

Words and Music by WALTER BECKER
and DONALD FAGEN

Moderately

In the ____ morn - in' you go gun - nin' for the ____ man ____
____ she's no high climb - er then you ____ find ____
____ and kick and beg ____ us that you're ____ not ____

____ who stole your wa - ter, ____ and you ____ fire ____
____ your on - ly friend ____ in a ____ room ____
____ a gam - blin' man; ____ then you ____ find ____

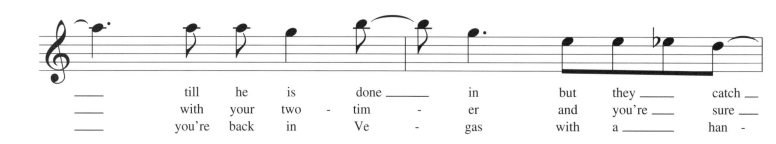

____ till he is done ____ in but they ____ catch ____
____ with your two - tim - er and you're ____ sure ____
____ you're back in Ve - gas with a ____ han -

____ you at the bor - der. And the ____ mourn -
____ you're near the end. ____ Then you ____ love ____
- dle in your hand. ____ Your black ____ cards ____

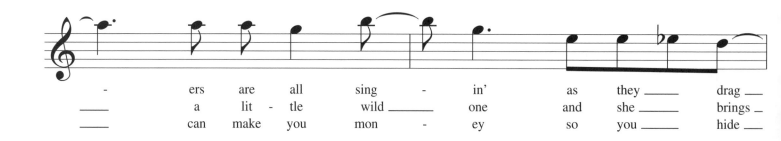

- ers are all sing - in' as they ____ drag ____
____ a lit - tle wild ____ one and she ____ brings ____
____ can make you mon - ey so you ____ hide ____

_____ you by your feet, _____ but the _____ hang -
_____ you on - ly sor - row; _____ all the _____ time __
_____ them when you're a - ble; _____ in the _____ land __

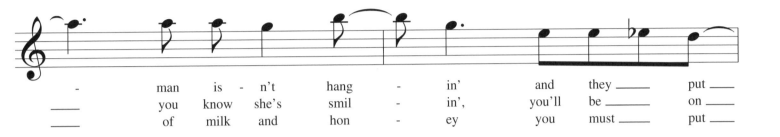

- man is - n't hang - in' and they _____ put __
_____ you know she's smil - in', you'll be _____ on __
_____ of milk and hon - ey you must _____ put __

Dm   Em

_____ you on the street. _____ ⎫ Yeah, __ you go back, Jack,
_____ your knees to - mor - row. ⎬
_____ them on the ta - ble. ⎭

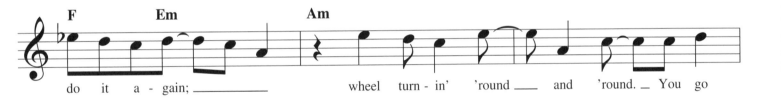

F   Em   Am

do it a - gain; _____ wheel turn - in' 'round __ and 'round. _ You go

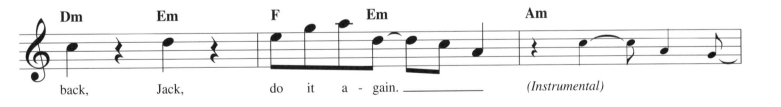

Dm   Em   F   Em   Am

back, Jack, do it a - gain. _____ _(Instrumental)_

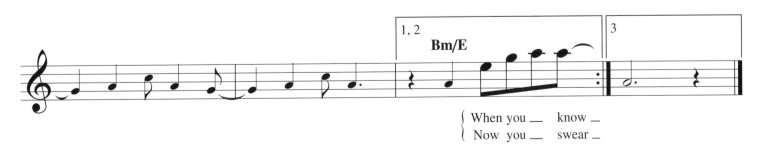

1, 2
Bm/E

3

⎧ When you __ know __
⎨ Now you __ swear __

DON'T BRING ME DOWN

Words and Music by
JEFF LYNNE

Moderately

You got me run - ning, go - ing out of my mind. ___
You want to stay out with your fan - cy friends. ___

You got me think - ing that I'm wast - ing my time.)
I'm tell - ing you it's got to be ___ the end.)   Don't bring me

down. ___   No, no, no, no, no. _____   Oo, ee, hoo. ___

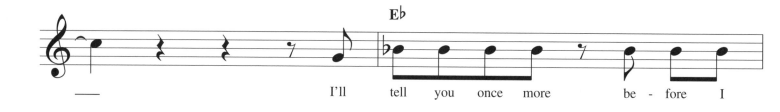

___   I'll tell you once more be - fore I

1
get off the floor.   Don't bring me down.

2
get off the floor.   Don't bring me down.

Don't bring me down. _____ Grrooss. __

___ Don't bring me down. _____ Grrooss. __ Don't bring me

down. ___ Grrooss. ___ Don't bring me down. _____

_____ What hap - pened to the girl I
You're al - ways talk - ing 'bout your

used to know? You let your mind out some - where
cra - zy nights. One of these days you're gon - na

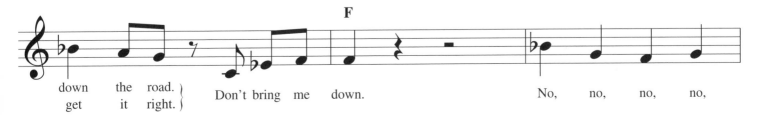

down the road.)
get it right.) Don't bring me down. No, no, no, no,

DON'T DO ME LIKE THAT

Words and Music by
TOM PETTY

DON'T FEAR THE REAPER

Words and Music by
DONALD ROESER

Moderately

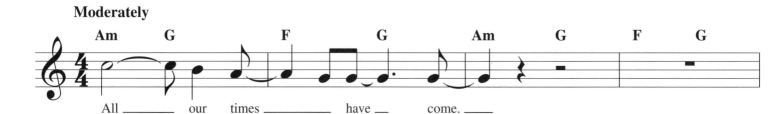

All ____ our times ____ have __ come. ____

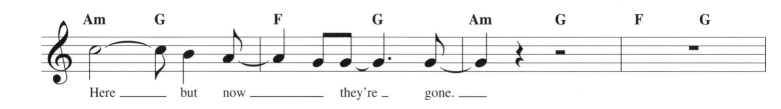

Here ____ but now ____ they're _ gone. ____

Sea - sons don't fear the reap - er, nor do the wind, the sun or the rain. __

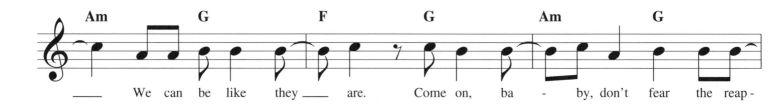

____ We can be like they ____ are. Come on, ba - by, don't fear the reap-

- er. Ba - by, take my hand. ____ Don't fear the reap - er. We'll be a - ble to fly. __

____ Don't fear the reap - er. Ba - by, I'm your man. ____

La, _____ la, la, _____ la, _____ la. _____

La, _____ la, la, _____ la, _____ la. _____

Val - en - tine _____ is _____ done. _____

Here _____ but now _____ they're _ gone. _____

Ro - me - o and Ju - li - et are to - geth - er in e - ter - ni - ty. _

_ For - ty thou - sand men and wom-en ev - 'ry day.

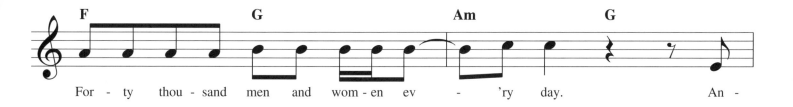

For - ty thou - sand men and wom-en ev - 'ry day. An -

oth - er for - ty thou - sand com - ing ev - 'ry day. Come on, ba -

- by. Ba - by, take my hand. ___ We'll be a - ble to fly. ___

___ Ba - by, I'm your man. ___

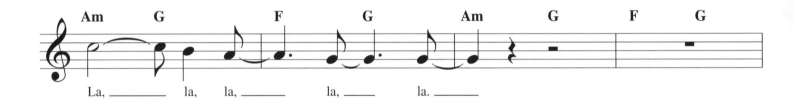

La, ___ la, la, ___ la, ___ la. ___

La, ___ la, la, ___ la, ___ la. ___

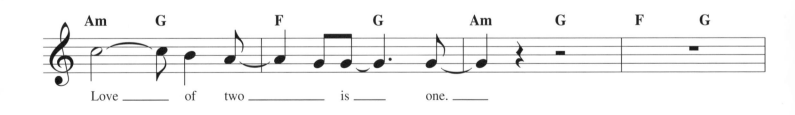

Love ___ of two ___ is ___ one. ___

Here ___ but now ___ they're ___ gone. ___

Came the last night of sad - ness, and it was clear she could -n't go on. _

_ And the door was o - pen and the wind __ a'peared. The

can - dles blew __ and then dis - ap-peared. The cur - tains flew __ and then he

ap-peared. Said don't be a - fraid. ___ Come on, ba - by. ___ And she had no fear. _

_ And she ran ___ to him. They looked back - ward and said _

___ good - bye. She had tak - en his hand. ___

Come on, ba - by. Don't fear the reap - er.

DON'T STAND SO CLOSE TO ME

Music and Lyrics by
STING

Steadily

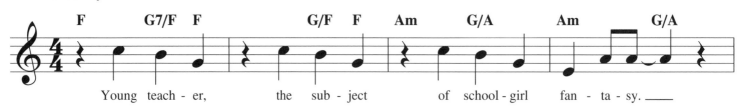

Young teach - er, the sub - ject of school - girl fan - ta - sy. __

She wants him so bad - ly, knows what she wants to be. __

In - side her there's long - ing. This girl's an o - pen page.

Book mark - ing, she's so close now. This girl is half his age. __

Don't stand, don't stand so, don't stand so close to me. __

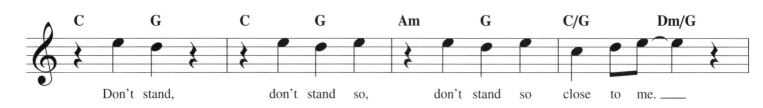

Don't stand, don't stand so, don't stand so close to me. __

Her friends __ are so jeal - ous; you know how
Loose talk __ in the class - room, to hurt they

Instrumental

DON'T STOP

Words and Music by
CHRISTINE McVIE

DOWN ON THE CORNER

Words and Music by
JOHN FOGERTY

Brightly, in 2

Ear - ly in the eve - nin' just a - bout sup - per time, ___
Roos - ter hits the wash - board and peo - ple just got to smile, ___
You don't need a pen - ny just to hang a - round, ___

___ o - ver by the court - house they're
___ Blink - y thumps the gut _____ bass and
___ but if you've got a nick - el, won't you

start - ing to un - wind. _____
so - los for a while. _____
lay your mon - ey down? ___

Four kids on the cor -
Poor - boy twangs the rhy -
O - ver on the cor -

- ner try - ing to bring you up. _____
- thm out on his kal - a - ma - zoo. _____
- ner there's a hap - py noise. _____

Wil - ly picks a tune ___
Wil - ly goes in - to ___
Peo - ple come from all ___

___ out and he blows it on the harp. ___
___ a dance and dou - bles on ka - zoo. ___
___ a - round to watch the mag - ic boy. ___

Down on the cor -

- ner, out in the street, ___ Wil - ly and the Poor - boys are play -

- in'. Bring a nick - el; tap your feet. ___

DREAM ON

Words and Music by
STEVEN TYLER

Moderately slow

Ev - 'ry time ___ that I look in the mir - ror, all these lines on my

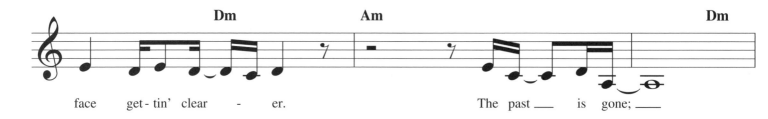

face get - tin' clear - er. The past ___ is gone; ___

it went by like ___ dusk to dawn. ___ Is - n't that the way ___

ev - 'ry - bod - y's got ___ their dues ___ in life ___ to pay? ___

___ I know no - bod - y knows where _ it comes and where _ it goes. _

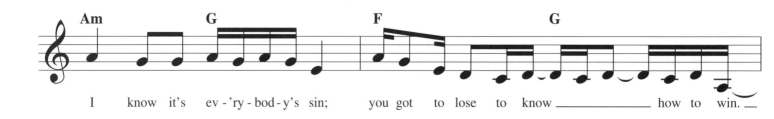

I know it's ev - 'ry - bod - y's sin; you got to lose to know ___ how to win. _

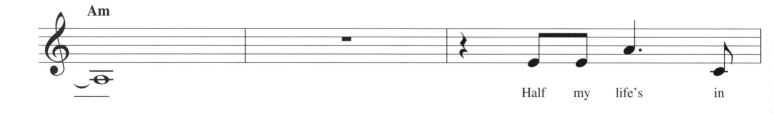

Half my life's in

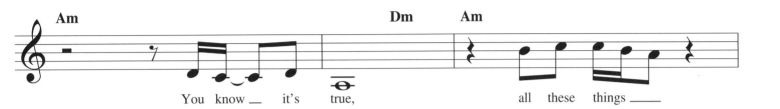

books' writ-ten pag - es,   lived and learned from fools and from sag - es.

You know __ it's   true,   all these things __

come back to you. _____   Sing with me, sing for the years, _

sing for the laugh-ter 'n' sing _____ for the tears. ____   Sing with me if it's just for to - day, _

may-be to-mor - row the good Lord __ will take you a - way. _____

Dream on, ___ dream on, ___ dream on, ___ dream your-self a dream come

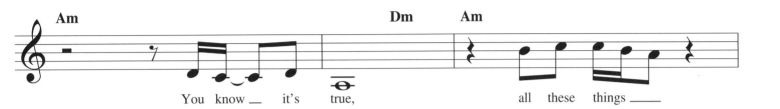

true. _____   *(Instrumental)*

84

Dream on, ___ dream on, ___ dream on ___ and dream un-til your dream comes

true. *(Instrumental)*

Dream on, ___ dream on, ___ dream on, ___ dream on. ___ Dream on, ___ dream on, ___

dream on, ___ ah. Ah. _____

Sing with me, sing for the years, ___ sing for the laugh-ter 'n' sing ___ for the tears. ___

Sing with me if it's just for to-day, ___ may-be to-mor-row the good Lord will take you a-way.

may-be to-mor-row the good Lord ___ will take you a-way.

HEY JOE

Words and Music by
BILLY ROBERTS

Moderately slow Rock

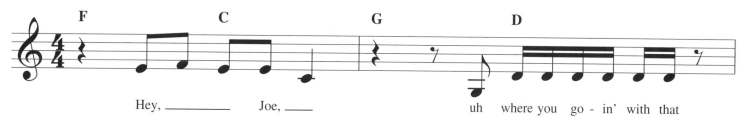

Hey, _____ Joe, _____ uh where you go - in' with that

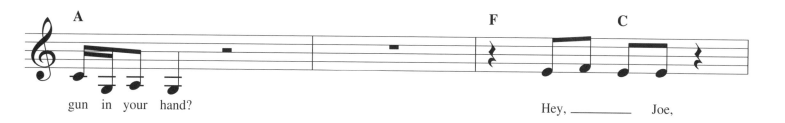

gun in your hand? Hey, _____ Joe,

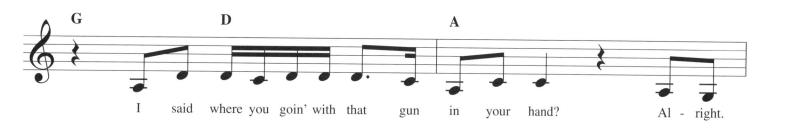

I said where you goin' with that gun in your hand? Al - right.

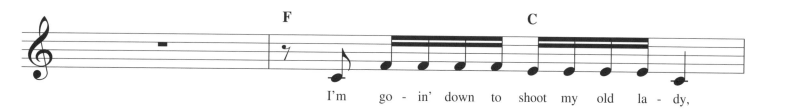

I'm go - in' down to shoot my old la - dy,

you know I caught her mess - in' 'round with an - oth - er man.

Yeah. I'm go - in' down to shoot my old la - dy,

86

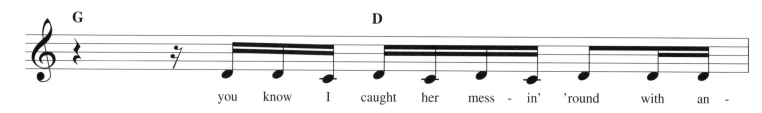

you know I caught her mess - in' 'round with an -

oth - er man.   Huh!   And that ain't too cool.

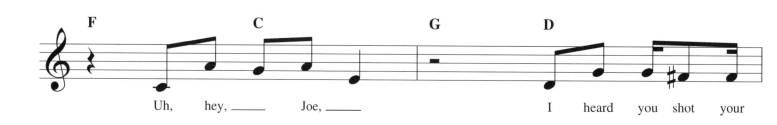

Uh, hey, ____ Joe, ____   I heard you shot your

wom - an down, __ you shot her down now. _____

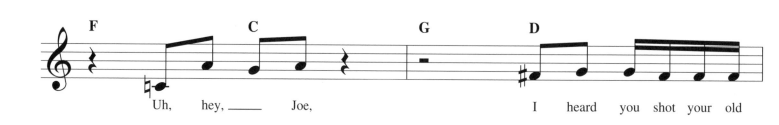

Uh, hey, ____ Joe,   I heard you shot your old

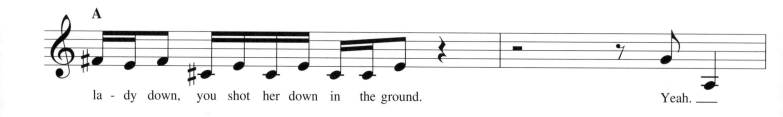

la - dy down, you shot her down in the ground.   Yeah. ____

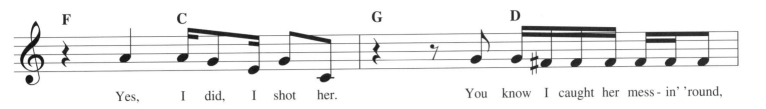

Yes, I did, I shot her. You know I caught her mess-in' 'round,

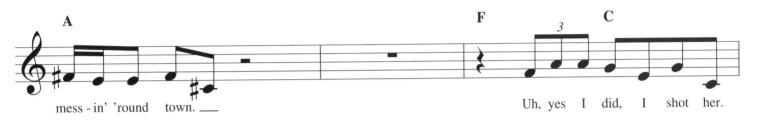

mess-in' 'round town. ___ Uh, yes I did, I shot her.

You know I caught my old la-dy mess-in' 'round

town. _____ And I gave her the gun. I shot her.

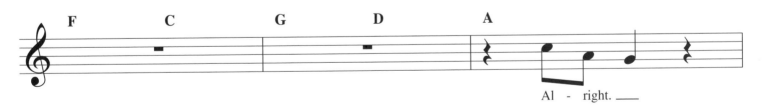

Al - right. ___

Shoot her one more time a - gain, ___ ba - by.

88

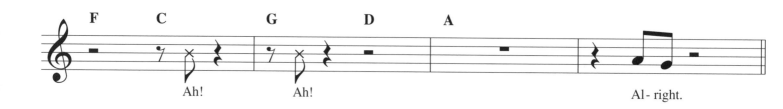

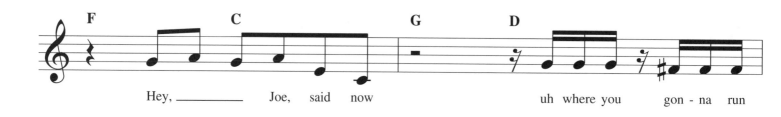

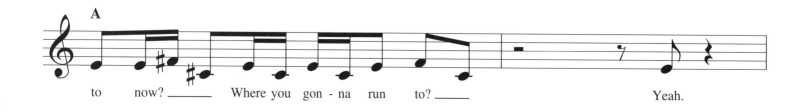

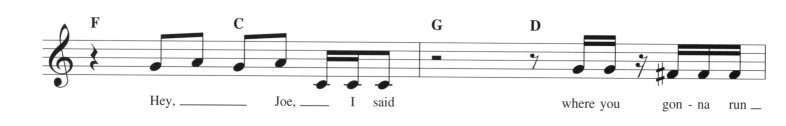

I'm go - in' way down south, ___ way down ___ to

Mex - i - co ___ way. ___ Al - right. ___

I'm go - in' way down south, ___ way ___ down where I ___

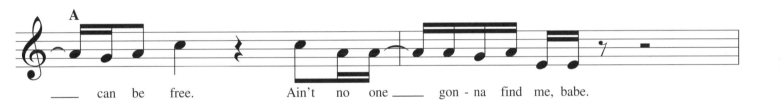

___ can be free. Ain't no one ___ gon - na find me, babe.

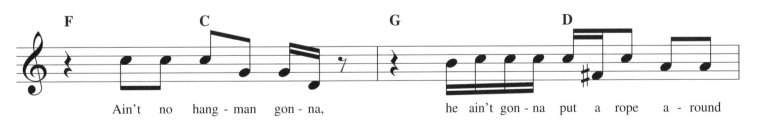

Ain't no hang - man gon - na, he ain't gon - na put a rope a - round

me. You bet - ter be - lieve ___ it right ___ now. ___ I got - ta go ___ now.

DRIVE MY CAR

Words and Music by JOHN LENNON
and PAUL McCARTNEY

Moderately, with a beat

Asked a girl what she want - ed to be.___
I told the girl that my pros - pects were good,___
I told that girl I could start right a - way,___

She said, "Ba - by, can't you see?___
and she said, "Ba - by, it's un - der - stood.___
and she said, "Lis-ten, babe, I got some - thing to say.

I wan - na be fa - mous, a star of the screen.___ But
Work - ing for pea - nuts is all ver - y fine.___ But
I got no car and it's break - ing my heart.___ But

you can do some - thing in be - tween:___
I can show you a bet - ter time:___
I found a driv - er, and that's a start:___

Ba - by, you can drive my car.___

Yes, I'm gon - na be a star.___

Ba - by, you can drive my car,___ and may - be I'll love___

EVERY LITTLE THING SHE DOES IS MAGIC

Music and Lyrics by
STING

1. Though I've tried be - fore to tell her of the feel -
2. *(See additional lyrics)*

- ings I have for her in ____ my ____ heart, ____

ev - 'ry time ____ that I come near her I just

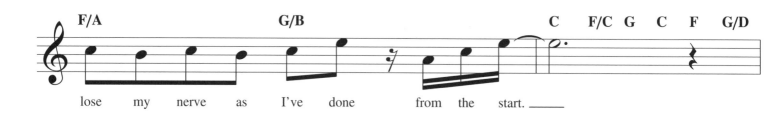

lose my nerve as I've done from the start. ____

Chorus

Ev - 'ry lit - tle thing she does is mag - ic, ev - 'ry - thing she

do just turns me on. E - ven though my life be - fore was trag - ic, now I know my

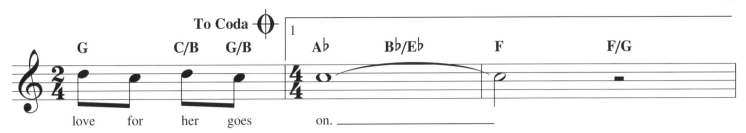

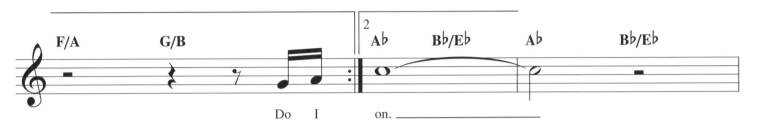

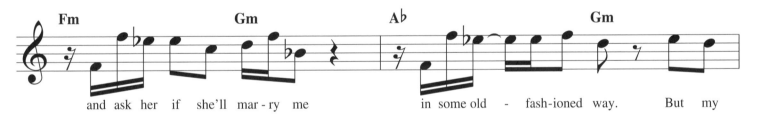

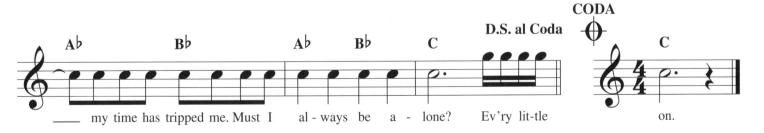

Additional Lyrics

2. Do I have to tell the story
   Of a thousand rainy days since we first met.
   It's a big enough umbrella
   But it's always me that ends up getting wet.
   Chorus

FREE BIRD

Words and Music by ALLEN COLLINS
and RONNIE VAN ZANT

Moderately

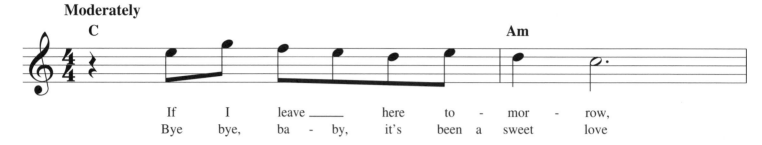

If   I   leave ____ here   to - mor - row,
Bye bye,   ba - by,   it's   been   a   sweet   love

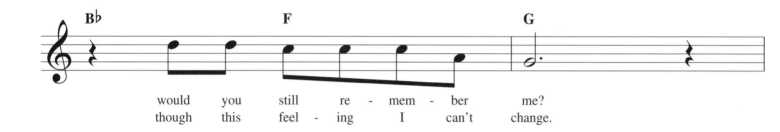

would   you   still   re - mem - ber   me?
though   this   feel - ing   I   can't   change.

For   I   must   be ____ trav - 'ling   on   now
But   please   don't   take ____ it   so   bad - ly

'cause   there's   too   man - y   plac - es   I've   got   to   see. ____
'cause   the   Lord   knows   I'm   to   blame. ____

But   if   I   stayed ____ here   with   you,   girl,

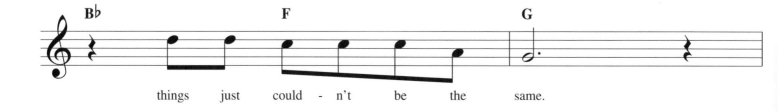

things   just   could - n't   be   the   same.

FREE RIDE

Words and Music by
DAN HARTMAN

With energy

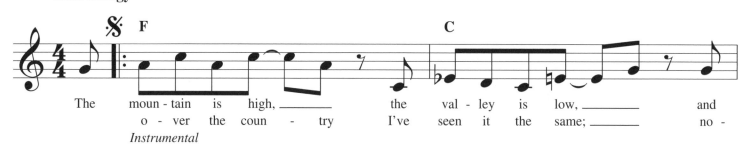

The moun - tain is high, _____ the val - ley is low, _____ and
o - ver the coun - try I've seen it the same; _____ no -
Instrumental

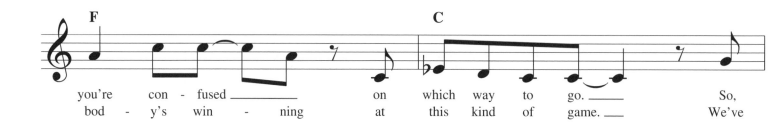

you're con - fused _____ on which way to go. _____ So,
bod - y's win - ning at this kind of game. __ We've

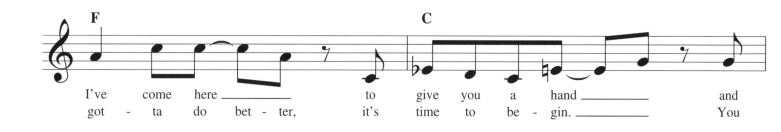

I've come here _____ to give you a hand _____ and
got - ta do bet - ter, it's time to be - gin. _____ You

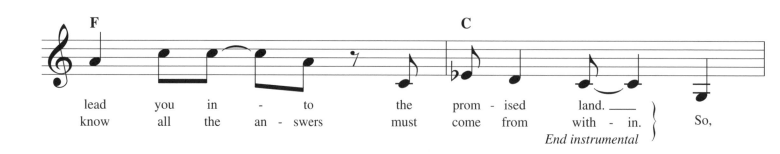

lead you in - to the prom - ised land. __
know all the an - swers must come from with - in. } So,
End instrumental

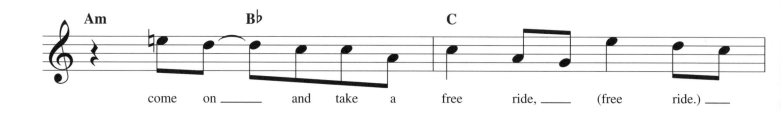

come on _____ and take a free ride, _____ (free ride.) __

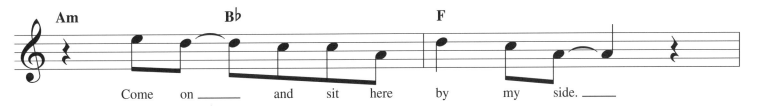

Come on _____ and sit here by my side. _____

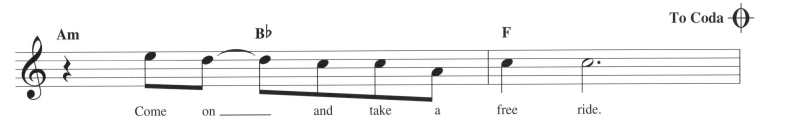

To Coda

Come on _____ and take a free ride.

(Instrumental)

D.S. al Coda

All Yeah, yeah, yeah, yeah.

CODA

Come on _____ and take a free ride. Yeah, yeah, yeah, yeah, yeah.

HEARTACHE TONIGHT

Words and Music by JOHN DAVID SOUTHER,
DON HENLEY, GLENN FREY and BOB SEGER

There's gon - na be a heart - ache to - night, a heart - ache to - night, I know.___

___ There's gon - na be a heart - ache to - night, a

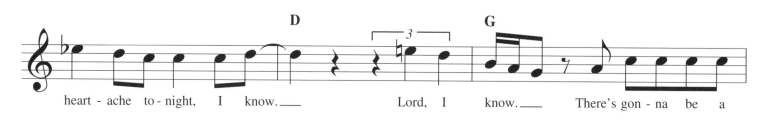

heart - ache to - night, I know.___ Lord, I know.___ There's gon - na be a

heart - ache to - night, the moon's shin - in' bright, so turn out the light, and

we'll get it right.___ There's gon - na be a heart - ache to - night,___ a

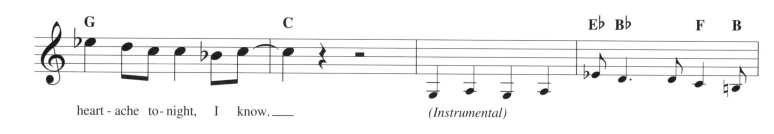

heart - ache to - night, I know.___ (Instrumental)

D.C. al Coda

CODA

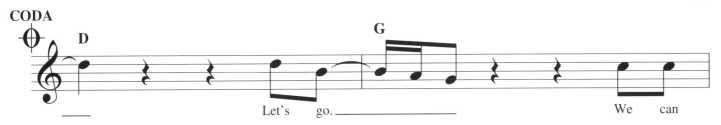

Let's go. _____ We can

beat a - round the bush - es; we can get down to the bone; we can

leave it in the park - in' lot, but ei - ther way, there's gon - na be a

heart - ache to - night, _____ a heart - ache to - night, I know. _

_____ Oh, I know. _____ There'll be a heart -

- ache to - night, _____ a heart - ache to - night, I know. ___

(Instrumental)

HIT ME WITH YOUR BEST SHOT

Words and Music by
EDDIE SCHWARTZ

Medium Rock

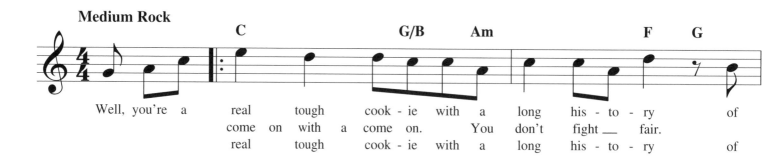

Well, you're a real tough cook - ie with a long his - to - ry of
come on with a come on. You don't fight __ fair.
real tough cook - ie with a long his - to - ry of

break - ing lit - tle hearts like the one in me.
But that's O - K. See if I care.
break - ing lit - tle hearts like the one in me. Be - fore I

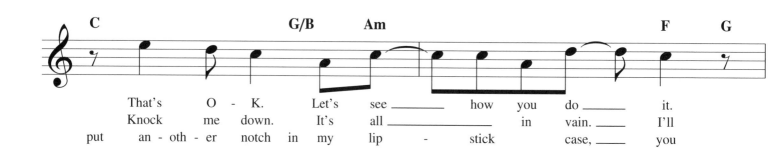

That's O - K. Let's see ___ how you do ___ it.
Knock me down. It's all ___ in vain. ___ I'll
put an - oth - er notch in my lip - stick case, ___ you

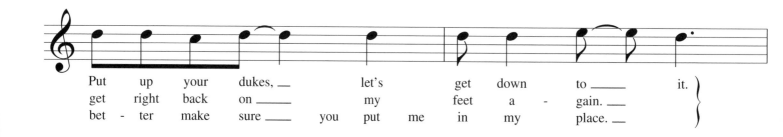

Put up your dukes, ___ let's get down to ___ it.
get right back on ___ my feet a - gain. ___
bet - ter make sure ___ you put me in my place. ___

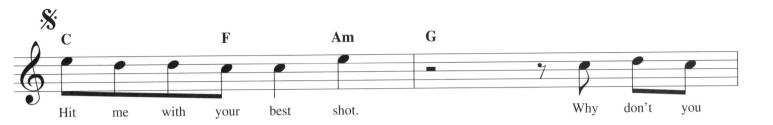

Hit me with your best shot. Why don't you

hit me with _____ your best shot? _____ *(Instrumental)*

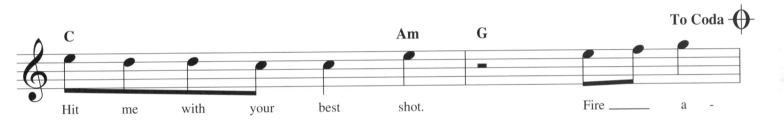

Hit me with your best shot. Fire _____ a-

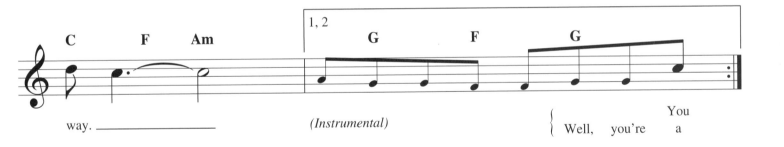

way. _____ *(Instrumental)*

| Well, you're a You

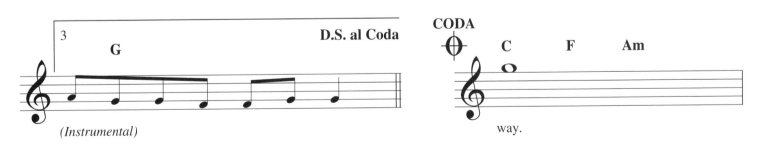

(Instrumental) D.S. al Coda

CODA way.

(Instrumental)

HOLD ON LOOSELY

Words and Music by JEFF CARLISI,
DON BARNES and JIM PETERIK

Moderately

You see it all a - round you: good __ lov - in' gone __
So damn   eas - y   when your feel - ings are __

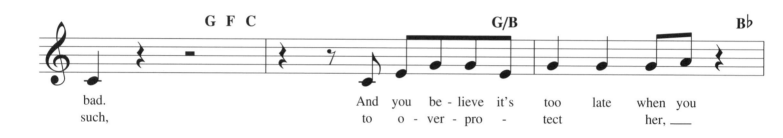

bad.   And you be - lieve it's too late when you
such,   to o - ver - pro - tect   her, __

re - al - ize what you had. _____   And my mind goes back __
to love her too much. _____

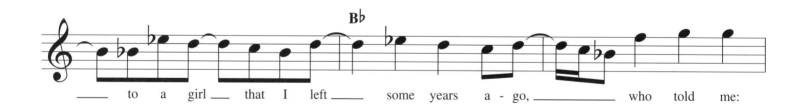

__ to a girl __ that I left __ some years a - go, _____ who told me:

Just hold on __ loose - ly,   but don't let __ go.

If you cling too tight - ly,

you're gon - na lose con - trol. Your ba - by needs some -

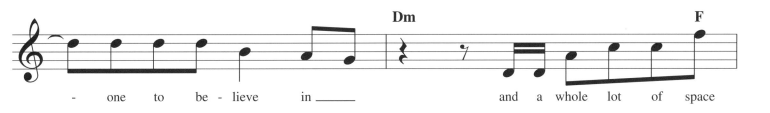

- one to be - lieve in and a whole lot of space

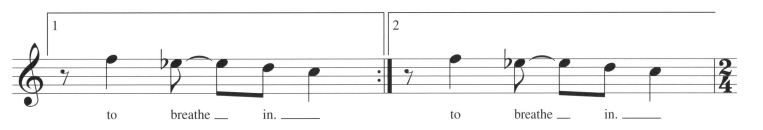

to breathe in. to breathe in.

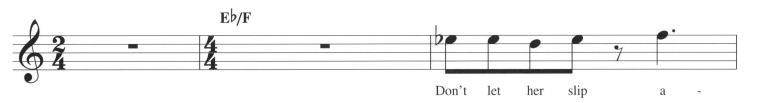

Don't let her slip a -

way. Sen - ti - men - tal fool.

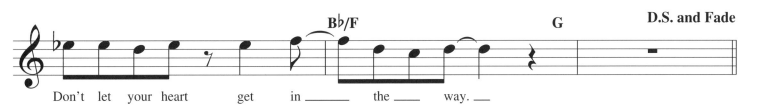

Don't let your heart get in the way.

HOT BLOODED

Words and Music by MICK JONES
and LOU GRAMM

Medium Rock beat

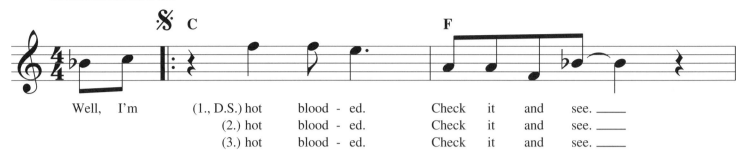

Well, I'm (1., D.S.) hot blood - ed. Check it and see. _____
(2.) hot blood - ed. Check it and see. _____
(3.) hot blood - ed. Check it and see. _____

I got a fe - ver of a hun - dred and three. _____
I got a fe - ver of a hun - dred and three. _____
I feel a fe - ver burn - in' in - side of me. _____

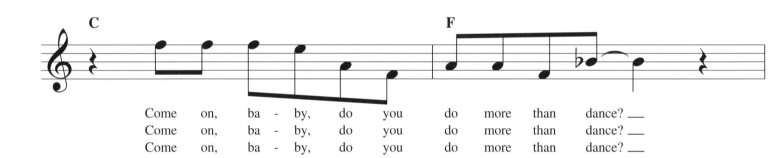

Come on, ba - by, do you do more than dance? _____
Come on, ba - by, do you do more than dance? _____
Come on, ba - by, do you do more than dance? _____

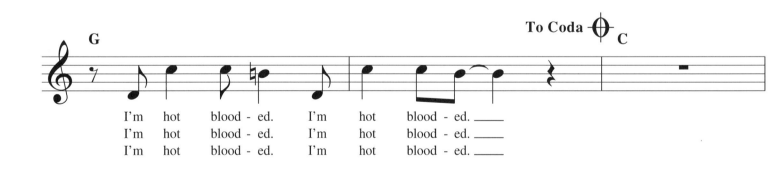

I'm hot blood - ed. I'm hot blood - ed. _____
I'm hot blood - ed. I'm hot blood - ed. _____
I'm hot blood - ed. I'm hot blood - ed. _____

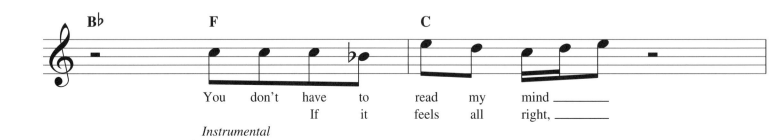

You don't have to read my mind _____
If it feels all right, _____

Instrumental

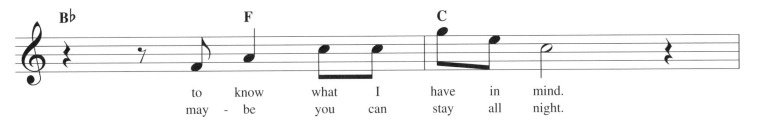

to know   what   I   have   in   mind.
may - be   you   can   stay   all   night.

Hon - ey,   you ought to   know. ___   Now, you
Should I   leave you my   key? ___   But you've got   to

move so ___   fine.   Let me   lay it on the line.
give me a   sign.   Come on, girl,   some   kind of sign.

               I   wan - na know   what you're do - in'   af - ter the show. ___
Tell me,   are you   hot, ma - ma?   You sure   look that way to

___   Now, it's   up   to   you. ___
me.   Are you old e - nough? ___
             End instrumental   Now, it's   up   to   you. ___

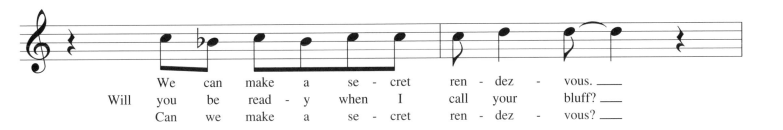

       We can make a se - cret   ren - dez - vous. ___
Will you be read - y when I call your bluff? ___
Can we make a se - cret   ren - dez - vous? ___

Just me and you; _____ I'll show you lov - in' like you
Is my tim - ing right? ___ Did you save your love for
Be - fore we do, _____ you'll have to get a - way from

1, 2 Bb G | **3** Bb G D.S. al Coda

nev - er knew. _ That's why I'm Well, I'm
me to - night? _ Yeah, I'm
you know who. _

CODA

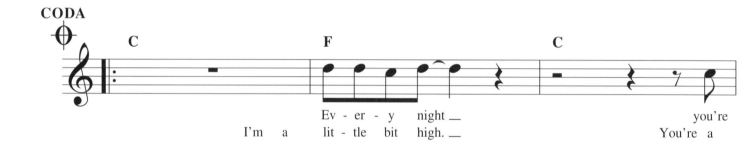

C | F | C

Ev - er - y night _ you're
I'm a lit - tle bit high. _ You're a

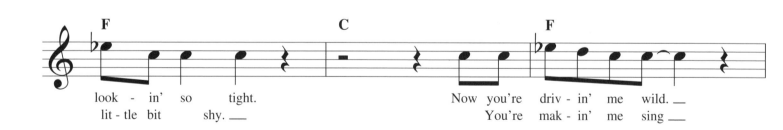

F | C | F

look - in' so tight. Now you're driv - in' me wild. _
lit - tle bit shy. _ You're mak - in' me sing _

G | **1** | **2** C

I'm so hot for you, child. _
for your sweet, sweet thing. _

HUSH

Words and Music by
JOE SOUTH

Driving Rock

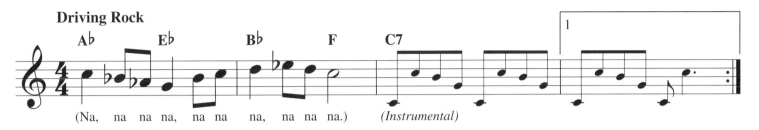

(Na, na na na, na na na, na na na.)   *(Instrumental)*

I got a cer-tain lit-tle girl, she's on __ my my mind.
She got __ lov-in' like __ quick-sand,

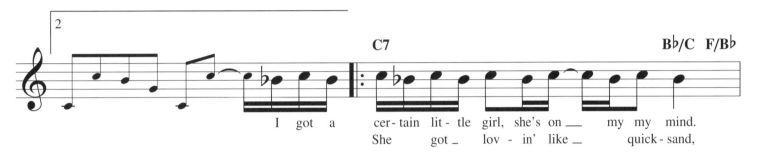

No doubt a-bout it, she looks _____ so fine.
On-ly took one touch _____ of her hand to

She's the best girl that I ev-er had. _____
blow my mind, and I'm in so deep that

Some-time, she gon-na make me feel so bad.
I can't eat, y'all, and I can't sleep.   (Na, na na na, na na

na, na na na.)   *(Instrumental)*

(Na, na na na, na na na, na na na.)　　　(Instrumental)

Hush, ___ hush. ___ I

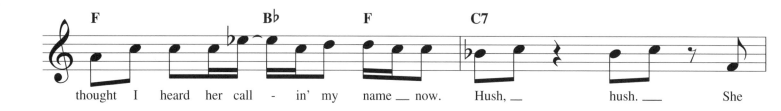

thought I heard her call - in' my name ___ now. Hush, ___ hush. ___ She

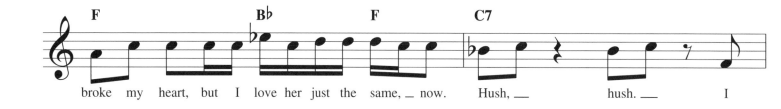

broke my heart, but I love her just the same, ___ now. Hush, ___ hush. ___ I

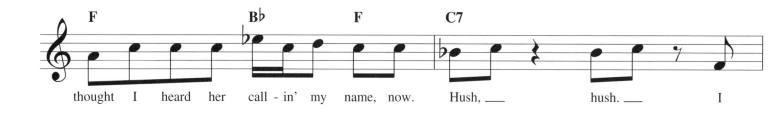

thought I heard her call - in' my name, now. Hush, ___ hush. ___ I

need her lov - in' and I'm _____ not to blame, ___ now.

(Love, love.) ___ We got it ear - ly in the morn - ing.

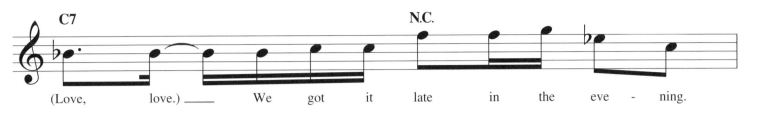

(Love, love.) _____ We got it late in the eve - ning.

(Love, love.) _____ Uh well, I want and need it.

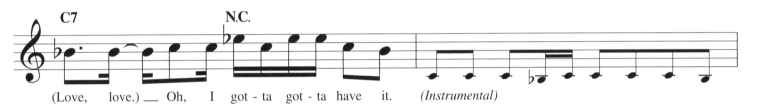

(Love, love.) _ Oh, I got - ta got - ta have it. *(Instrumental)*

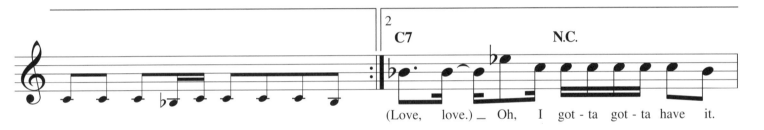

(Love, love.) _ Oh, I got - ta got - ta have it.

(Na, na na na, na na na, na na na.)

(Na, na na na, na na na, na na na.) (Na, na na

na, na na na, na na na.)

HURTS SO GOOD

Words and Music by JOHN MELLENCAMP
and GEORGE GREEN

Moderate Rock

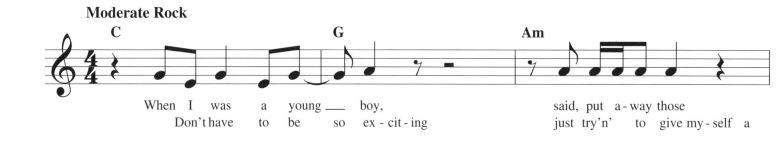

When I was a young ___ boy, said, put a-way those
Don't have to be so ex-cit-ing just try'n' to give my-self a

young boy ways. Now that I'm get-tin' old-er, so much old-er,
lit-tle bit of fun, yeah. You al-ways look so ___ in-vit-ing.

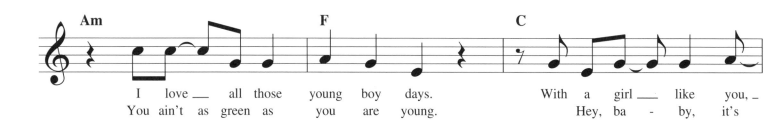

I love ___ all those young boy days. With a girl ___ like you, ___
You ain't as green as you are young. Hey, ba-by, it's

___ you. with a girl ___ like you, ___
you. Come on, girl, ___ now, it's you. ___

Lord knows, there are things ___ we can do, ___ ba-by, just me and you.
Sink your teeth right through ___ my ___ bones, ___ ba-by. Let's see what we can do.

___ Come on and make it
___ Come on and make it   hurt so good. ___

Come on, ba - by, make it hurt so good. Some-times love ___ don't

feel like it should. _ You make it hurt so good. ___ *(Instrumental)*

I ain't talk - in' no big ___ deals; I ain't made no plans _

___ my - self. I ain't talk - in' no high ___ heels. May - be we could

walk a - round all ___ day long, walk a - round all ___ day long,

___ *(Instrumental)*

I SHOT THE SHERIFF

Words and Music by
BOB MARLEY

Moderately slow, with a beat

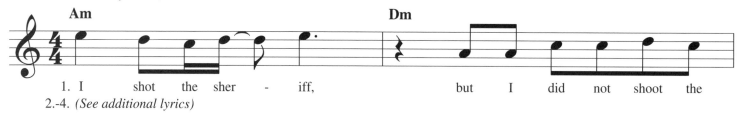

1. I shot the sher - iff, but I did not shoot the
2.-4. *(See additional lyrics)*

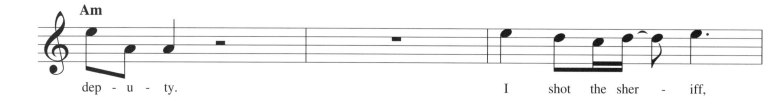

dep - u - ty. I shot the sher - iff,

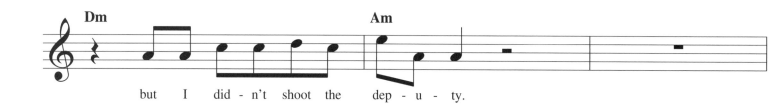

but I did - n't shoot the dep - u - ty.

All a - round in my home town, they're try - ing to track me down.

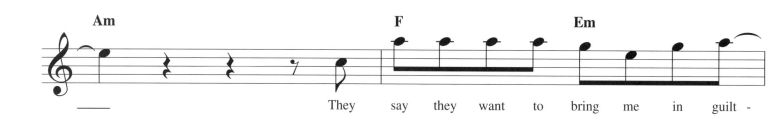

They say they want to bring me in guilt -

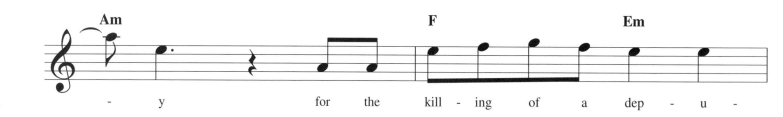

- y for the kill - ing of a dep - u -

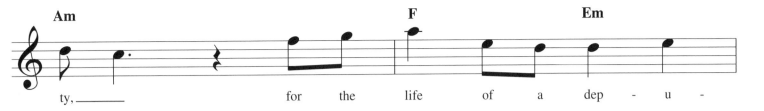

ty,_____ for the life of a dep - u -

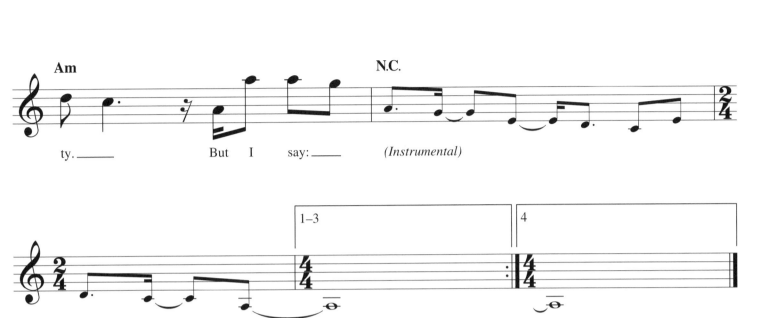

ty._____ But I say:_____ *(Instrumental)*

1–3   4

Additional Lyrics

2. I shot the sheriff, but I swear it was in self-defense.
   I shot the sheriff, and they say it is a capital offense.
   Sheriff John Brown always hated me; for what, I don't know.
   Every time that I plant a seed, he said, "Kill it before it grows."
   He said, "Kill it before it grows." But I say:

3. I shot the sheriff, but I swear it was in self-defense.
   I shot the sheriff, but I swear it was in self-defense.
   Freedom came my way one day, and I started out of town.
   All of a sudden, I see Sheriff John Brown aiming to shoot me down.
   So I shot, I shot him down. But I say:

4. I shot the sheriff, but I did not shoot the deputy.
   I shot the sheriff, but I didn't shoot the deputy.
   Reflexes got the better of me, and what is to be must be.
   Every day, the bucket goes to the well, but one day the bottom will drop out.
   Yes, one day the bottom will drop out. But I say:

IN THE AIR TONIGHT

Words and Music by
PHIL COLLINS

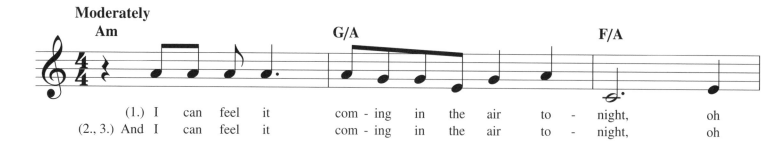

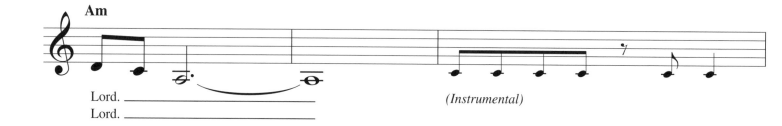

Well, if you told me ____ you were drown-ing ____ I
Well, I re - mem-ber, ____ I re - mem-ber, ____ don't wor - ry.

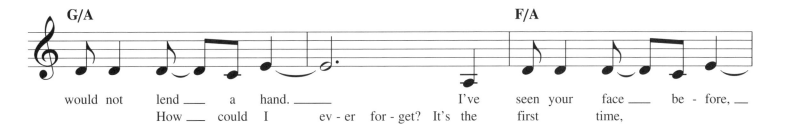

G/A   F/A

would not lend ____ a hand. ____ I've seen your face ____ be - fore, ____
How ____ could I ev - er for - get? It's the first time,

Am

____ my friend, but I don't know if you know ____ who I am. Well,
the last time we ev - er met. But I

G/A

I was there ____ and I saw what you did, ____ I saw it with my own two
know the rea - son why you keep the si - lence up. No, you don't

F/A

eyes. ____ So you can wipe off that grin, ____ I know where you've been, ____ it's
fool me. The hurt does - n't show, ____ but pain ____ still grows. ____ It's no

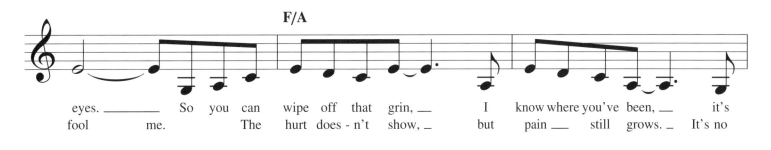

Am   1   2   D.C. al Coda

all been a pack ____ of lies. ____
stran - ger to you ____ or me. ____

CODA

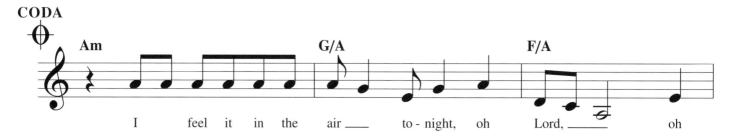

I feel it in the air ____ to - night, oh Lord, ____ oh

Lord. ____ Well, I've been wait - ing for this mo - ment for all my

life, oh Lord. ____ And I can feel it

com - ing in the air to - night, oh Lord, ____

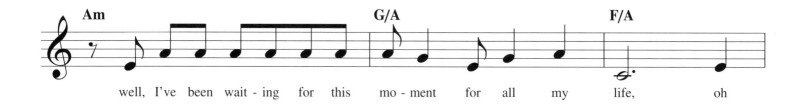

well, I've been wait - ing for this mo - ment for all my life, oh

Lord. ____ *(Instrumental)*

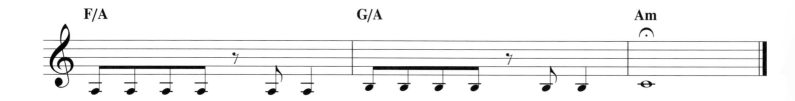

I LOVE ROCK 'N ROLL

Words and Music by ALAN MERRILL
and JAKE HOOKER

I saw him danc - ing there ____ by the rec - ord ma -
smiled, so I got up ____ and asked ____ for his

chine.
name.

I knew he must have been ____
"That don't mat - ter," he

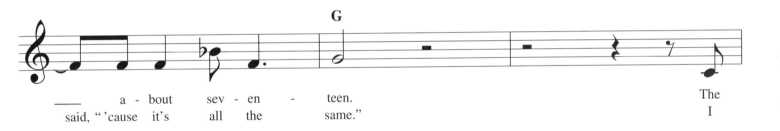

____ a - bout sev - en - teen.
said, " 'cause it's all the same."

The
I

beat was go - ing strong, ____
said, "Can I take you home ____

play - ing my fa - v'rite
where we can be a -

song,
lone?"

and I could tell it would - n't be long ____
And next, we were mov - ing

till he was with me, yeah, me. And I could
on, and he was with me, yeah, me. And

tell it would-n't be long ___ till he was with me, yeah,
next, we were mov-ing on, and he was with me, yeah,

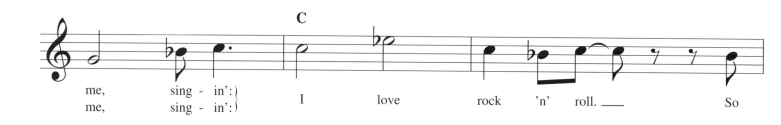

me, sing - in':} I love rock 'n' roll. ___ So
me, sing - in':}

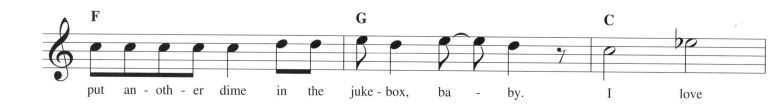

put an - oth - er dime in the juke - box, ba - by. I love

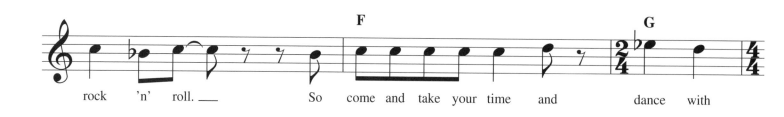

rock 'n' roll. ___ So come and take your time and dance with

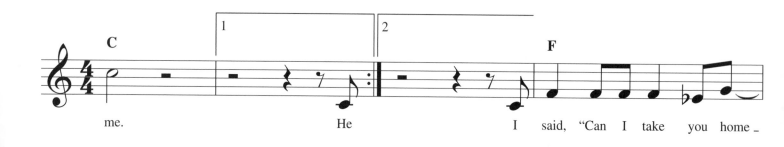

me. He
I said, "Can I take you home ___

where we can be a - lone?"

Next, we were mov - in' on, _____ and he was with me, yeah,

me. And we'll be mov - in' on _____ and sing - in' that same old

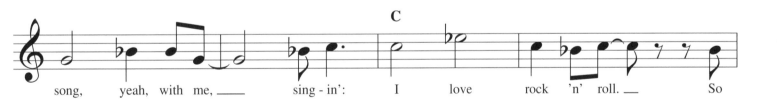

song, yeah, with me, _____ sing - in': I love rock 'n' roll. _____ So

put an - oth - er dime in the juke - box, ba - by. I love

rock 'n' roll. _____ So come and take your time and dance with me.

JACK AND DIANE

Words and Music by
JOHN MELLENCAMP

Moderately, in 2

A lit - tle dit - ty a - bout Jack and Di - ane, __

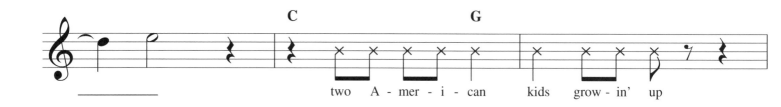

__ two A - mer - i - can kids grow - in' up

in the heart - land. Jack, he's gon - na be __ a

foot - ball star; _____ Di - ane deb - u -

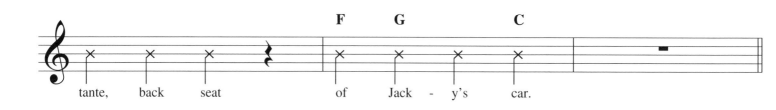

tante, back seat of Jack - y's car.

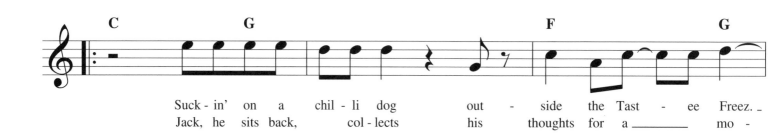

Suck - in' on a chil - li dog out - side the Tast - ee Freez.
Jack, he sits back, col - lects his thoughts for a __ mo -

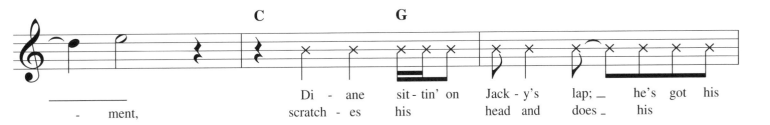

- ment,

C   G

Di - ane   sit - tin' on   Jack - y's   lap;   he's got his
scratch - es   his   head and   does   his

F   G   C   G

hands   be - tween   her knees.   Jack, he says, "Hey,
best   James   Dean: "Well, then, there,

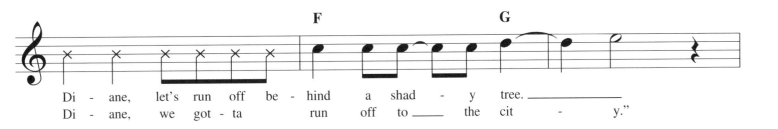

F   G

Di - ane,   let's run off be - hind   a shad - y tree. _____
Di - ane,   we got - ta   run off to ____ the cit - y."

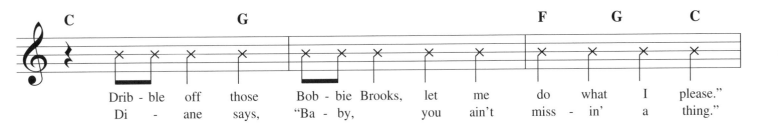

C   G   F   G   C

Drib - ble off those   Bob - bie Brooks, let me   do what I   please."
Di - ane says,   "Ba - by,   you ain't   miss - in' a   thing."

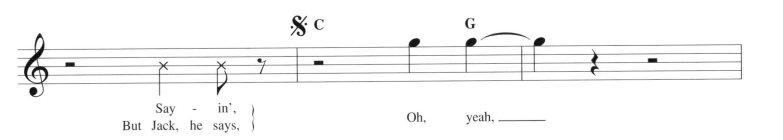

𝄋 C   G

Say - in',   Oh,   yeah, _____
But Jack, he says,

F   G   C   G

life   goes ___ on, _____   long af - ter the

124

thrill of liv - ing is _____ gone. _____ Say - in',

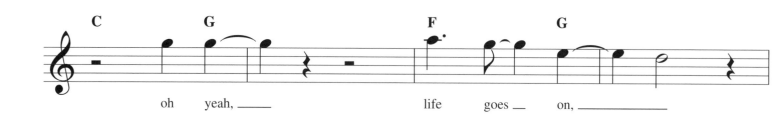

oh yeah, _____ life goes _ on, _____

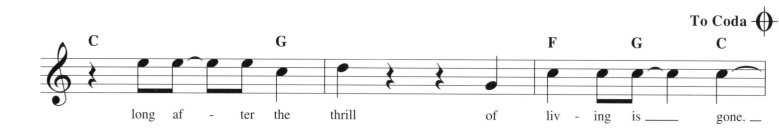

long af - ter the thrill of liv - ing is _____ gone. _

_____ Now, walk on. _____ Oh, let it rock,

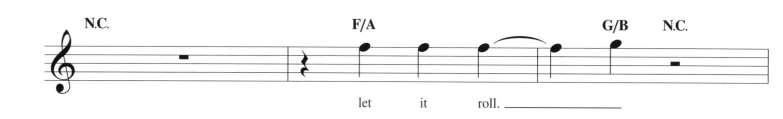

let it roll. _____

Let the Bi - ble belt come and save my soul. _

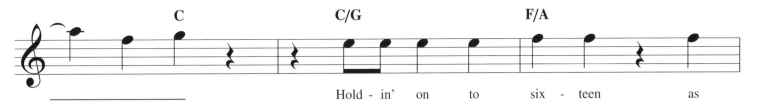

C   C/G   F/A

_____ Hold - in' on to six - teen as

B♭   F/A   C   N.C.   C/G

long as you can. _____ Change is com - in' 'round

F/A   G   C   N.C.   **D.S. al Coda**

real soon, make us wom - en and men.

CODA   G

__ A lit - tle dit - ty a - bout

F   G   C   G

Jack and Di - ane, _____ two A - mer - i - can

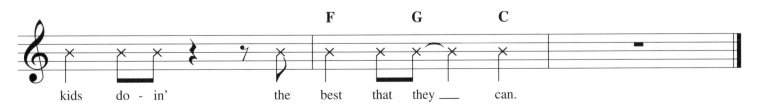

    F   G   C

kids do - in' the best that they __ can.

JET AIRLINER

Words and Music by
PAUL PENA

Moderate Rock beat

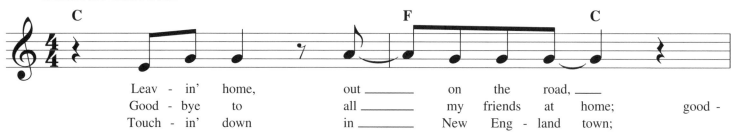

Leav - in' home, out _____ on the road, _____
Good - bye to all _____ my friends at home; good -
Touch - in' down in _____ New Eng - land town;

I've been down be - fore. _____ I've
- bye to peo - ple I've trust - ed. _____ I've
feel the heat com - in' down. _____ I've

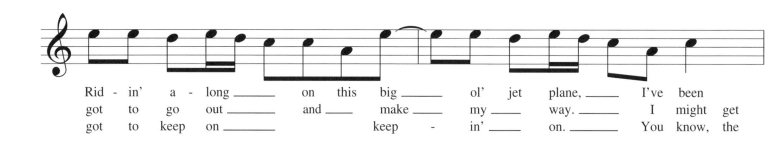

Rid - in' a - long _____ on this big _____ ol' jet plane, _____ I've been
got to go out _____ and _____ make _____ my _____ way. _____ I might get
got to keep on _____ keep - in' _____ on. _____ You know, the

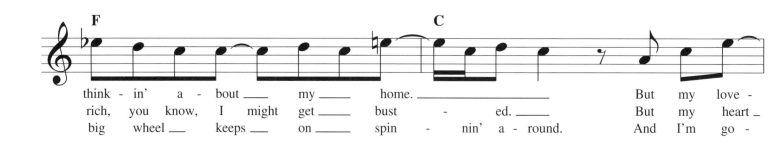

think - in' a - bout _____ my _____ home. _____ But my love -
rich, you know, I might get _____ bust - ed. _____ But my heart _____
big wheel _____ keeps _____ on _____ spin - nin' a - round. And I'm go -

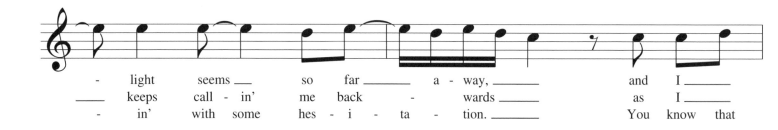

- light seems _____ so far _____ a - way, _____ and I _____
_____ keeps call - in' me back - wards _____ as I _____
- in' with some hes - i - ta - tion. _____ You know that

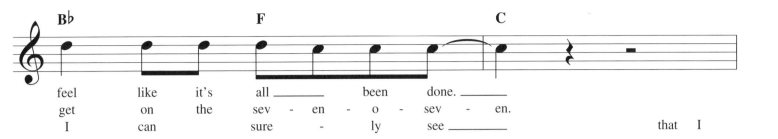

feel like it's all _____ been done. _____
get on the sev - en - o - sev - en.
I can sure - ly see _____ that I

Some - bod - y's try'n' ___ to make _____ me stay. _____ You know, I've
Rid - in' high, ___ I got tears in my ___ eyes. You know, you
don't want to get caught up in an - y of _____ that

got to be mov - in' on. Oh. _____
got to go through hell be - fore you get to heav - en.
funk - y shit go - in' down in the cit - y.

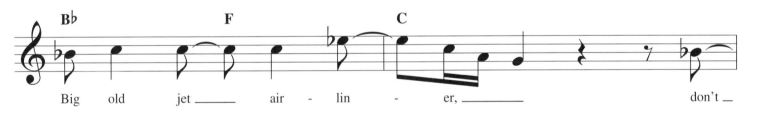

Big old jet _____ air - lin - er, _____ don't _

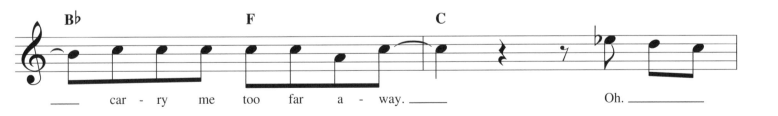

___ car - ry me too far a - way. _____ Oh. _____

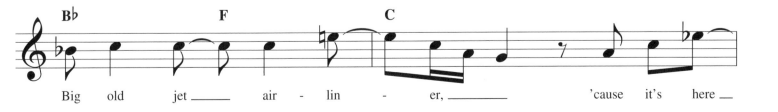

Big old jet _____ air - lin - er, _____ 'cause it's here _

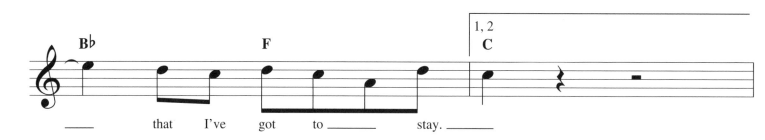

that I've got to _____ stay. _____

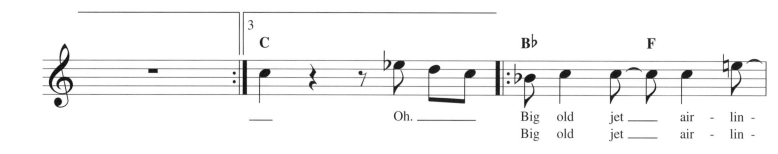

_____ Oh. _____ Big old jet _____ air - lin -
Big old jet _____ air - lin -

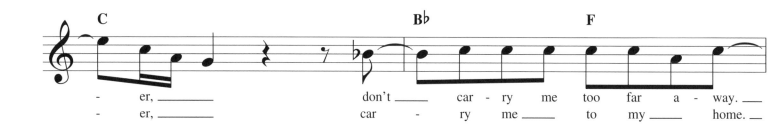

- er, _____ don't _____ car - ry me too far a - way. _____
- er, _____ car - ry me _____ to my _____ home. _____

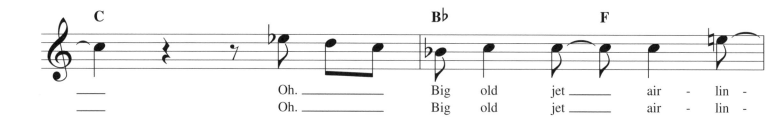

_____ Oh. _____ Big old jet _____ air - lin -
_____ Oh. _____ Big old jet _____ air - lin -

- er, _____ 'cause it's here _____ that I've got to _____ stay. _____
- er, _____ 'cause it's there _____ that _____ I be - long. _____

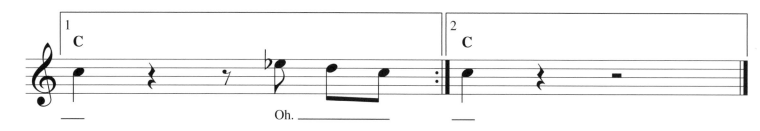

_____ Oh. _____ _____

LAYLA

Words and Music by ERIC CLAPTON
and JIM GORDON

Moderately fast Rock

What will you do when you get lone - ly ___
I tried to give you con - so - la - tion ___
So make the best of the sit - u - a - tion ___

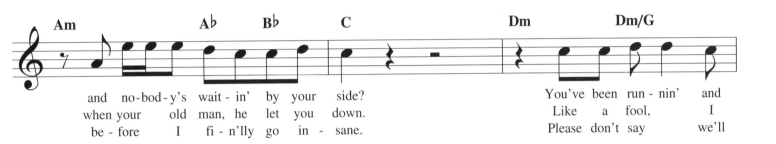

and no-bod-y's wait-in' by your side?
when your old man, he let you down.
be - fore I fi - n'lly go in - sane.
You've been run - nin' and
Like a fool, I
Please don't say we'll

hid - in' much too long; ___
fell in love with you; ___
nev - er find a way, ___
you know it's just your fool - ish pride.
you turned my whole world up - side down.
and tell me that my love's _ in vain.
Lay -

la, ___ you got me on my knees. Lay - la, ___ I'm

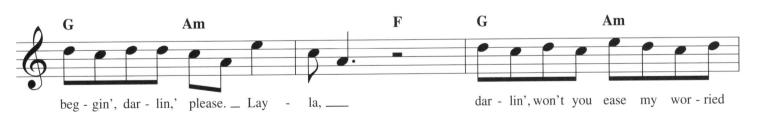

beg - gin', dar - lin,' please. _ Lay - la, ___ dar - lin', won't you ease my wor - ried

To Coda
1, 2
3
D.S. al Coda
CODA

mind? _ (Instrumental)
Lay -

JOY TO THE WORLD

Words and Music by
HOYT AXTON

Moderate Gospel Rock

Jer - e - mi - ah was a bull - frog,
If I were the king of the world,
know I love the la - dies,

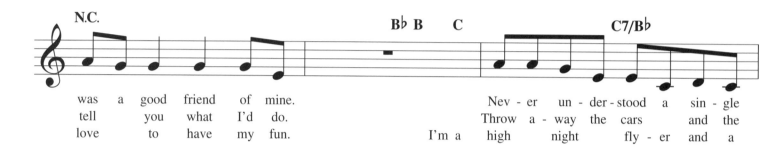

was a good friend of mine.
tell you what I'd do.
love to have my fun.

Nev - er un - der - stood a sin - gle
Throw a - way the cars and the
I'm a high night fly - er and a

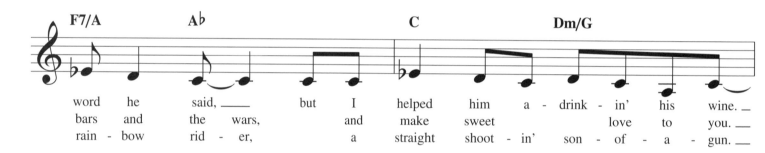

word he said, _____ but I helped him a - drink - in' his wine. _
bars and the wars, and make sweet love to you. _
rain - bow rid - er, a straight shoot - in' son - of - a - gun. _

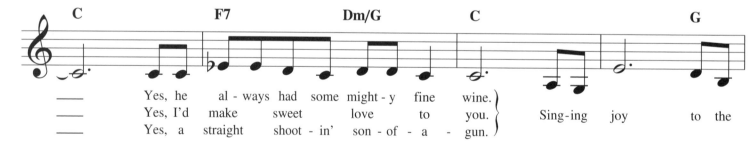

_____ Yes, he al - ways had some might - y fine wine.)
_____ Yes, I'd make sweet love to you. }
_____ Yes, a straight shoot - in' son - of - a - gun.)

Sing-ing joy to the

world, all _____ the boys and girls _ now.
Joy to the fish - es in the

To Coda ⊕

1.

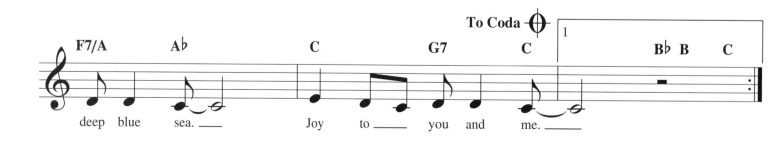

deep blue sea. _
Joy to _____ you and me. _

LA GRANGE

Words and Music by BILLY F GIBBONS,
DUSTY HILL and FRANK LEE BEARD

Moderately fast

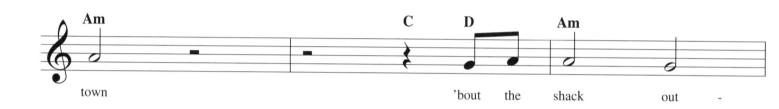

Ru - mors __ spread-ing 'round __ in that Tex - as

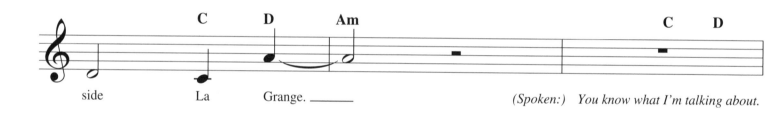

town 'bout the shack out -

side La Grange. _____ *(Spoken:) You know what I'm talking about.*

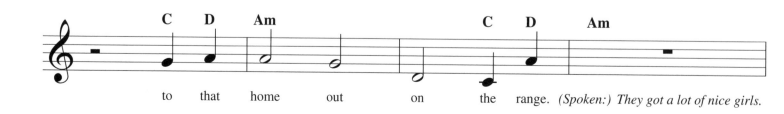

Just let me know if you __ wan - na go

to that home out on the range. *(Spoken:) They got a lot of nice girls.*

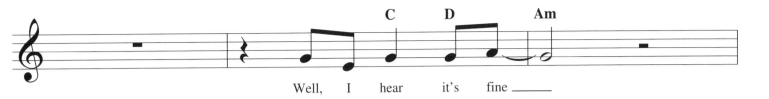

Well, I hear it's fine _____

if you've got the time _____ and the

ten to get _____ your - self in. _____

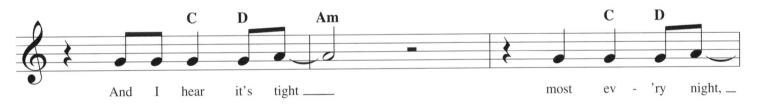

And I hear it's tight _____ most ev - 'ry night, __

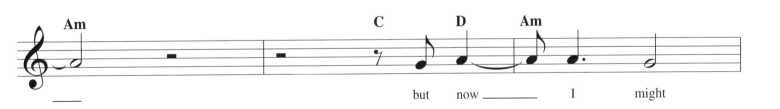

____ but now _____ I might

be mis - tak - en. _____ Hm, hm, hm.

LIVIN' ON A PRAYER

Words and Music by JON BON JOVI,
DESMOND CHILD and RICHIE SAMBORA

Moderate Rock

Tom-my used to work on the docks. _____ Un-ion's been on strike, he's
Tom-my's got his six-string in hock, _____ now he's hold-ing in what he

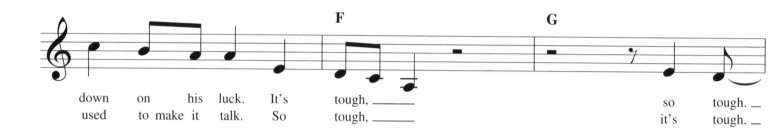

down on his luck. It's tough, _____ so tough. __
used to make it talk. So tough, _____ it's tough. __

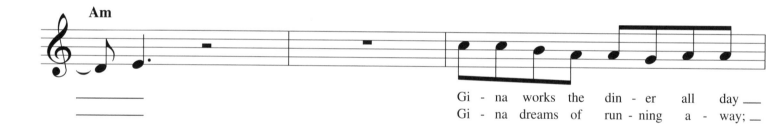

_____ Gi-na works the din-er all day __
_____ Gi-na dreams of run-ning a-way; __

_____ work-ing for her man. She brings home her pay, for
_____ when she cries in the night, Tom-my whis-pers: Ba-by, it's

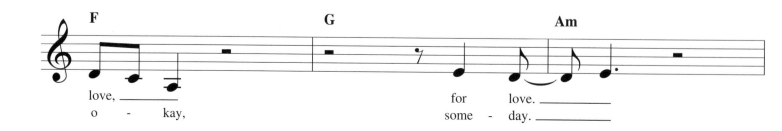

love, _____ for love. _____
o-kay, some-day. _____

Oh, _____ we've got to hold _____ on, _____

read - y or _____ not, you live for the fight when it's

all that you've got. Whoa, _____ we're half - way there. _____

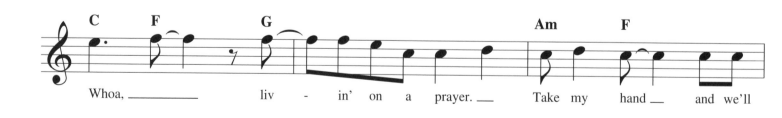

Whoa, _____ liv - in' on a prayer. _____ Take my hand _____ and we'll

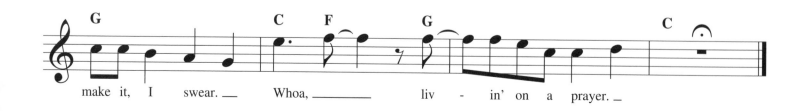

make it, I swear. _____ Whoa, _____ liv - in' on a prayer. _____

LONG COOL WOMAN
(In a Black Dress)

Words and Music by ALLAN CLARKE,
ROGER COOK and ROGER GREENAWAY

LORELEI

Words and Music by DENNIS DeYOUNG
and JAMES YOUNG

Moderately fast

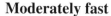

When I think of Lo - re - lei, ___ my head turns all a - round. ___
eyes be - come a par - a - dise, ___ she soft - ly speaks my name. ___

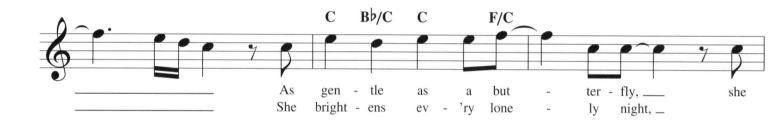

___ As gen - tle as a but - ter - fly, ___ she
___ She bright - ens ev - 'ry lone - ly night, ___

moves with - out a sound. ___ I call her on the tel -
no one's quite the same. ___ She calls me on the tel -

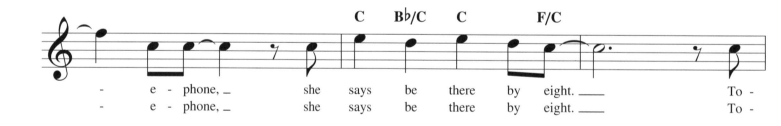

- e - phone, _ she says be there by eight. ___ To -
- e - phone, _ she says be there by eight. ___ To -

night's the night she's mov - in' in, ___ and I can hard - ly wait.
night's the night she's mov - in' in, ___ it's time to cel - e - brate. ___

___ The way she moves, _ ooh, ___

MAGIC CARPET RIDE

Words and Music by JOHN KAY
and RUSHTON MOREVE

Heavy Metal Rock

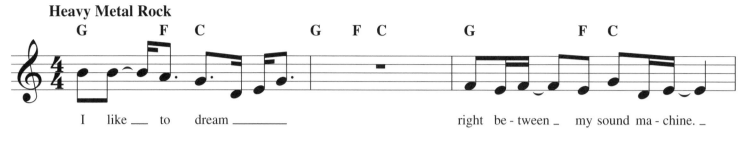

I like to dream right be-tween my sound ma-chine.

On a cloud of sound I drift in the night,

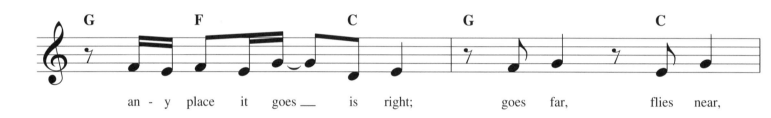

an - y place it goes is right; goes far, flies near,

to the stars a - way from here. Well, you don't know what

we can find. Oh, why don't you come with me, lit - tle girl,

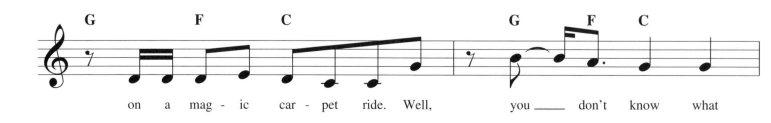

on a mag - ic car - pet ride. Well, you don't know what

we can see. Why don't you tell your dreams to me,

fan - tas - y ____ will set you free. Close your eyes, girl, look in - side, girl,

let the sound take you a - way. Last

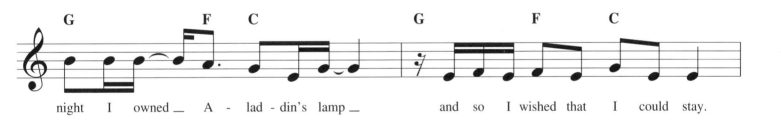

night I owned __ A - lad - din's lamp __ and so I wished that I could stay.

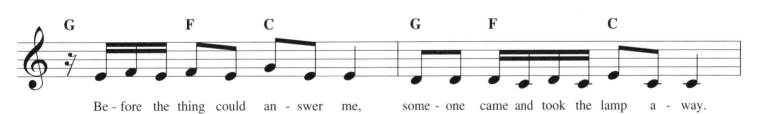

Be - fore the thing could an - swer me, some - one came and took the lamp a - way.

I looked a - round, a lous - y can - dle is all I found. Well,

MAGIC MAN

Words and Music by ANN WILSON
and NANCY WILSON

Moderate Rock beat

Cold late night so long a-go, when I was not so strong, you know, a
Win-ter nights we sang in tune, played in-side the months of moon:

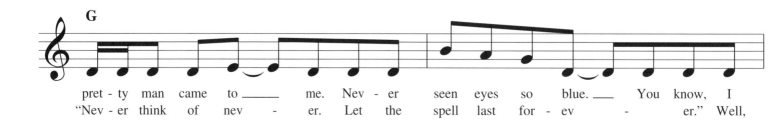

pret-ty man came to _____ me. Nev-er seen eyes so blue. ___ You know, I
"Nev-er think of nev - er. Let the spell last for-ev - er." Well,

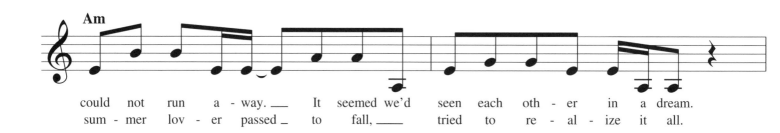

could not run a-way. ___ It seemed we'd seen each oth-er in a dream.
sum-mer lov-er passed _ to fall, ___ tried to re-al-ize it all.

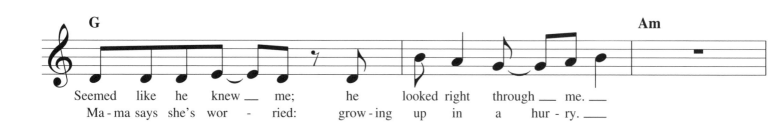

Seemed like he knew _ me; he looked right through _ me. _
Ma-ma says she's wor-ried: grow-ing up in a hur-ry. ___

"Come on ___ home, girl," he said with a smile. _
"Come on ___ home, _ girl," Ma-ma cried on the phone. "Too

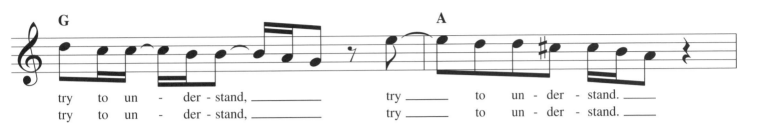

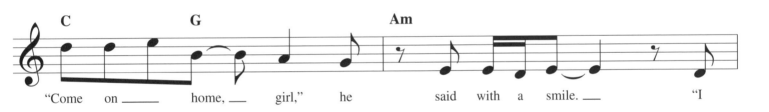

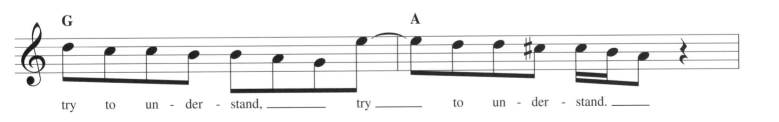

146

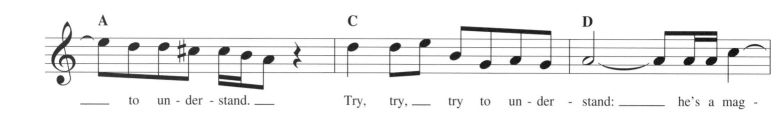

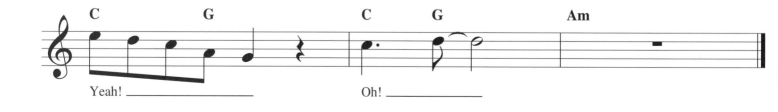

MAGGIE MAY

Words and Music by ROD STEWART
and MARTIN QUITTENTON

Moderately bright

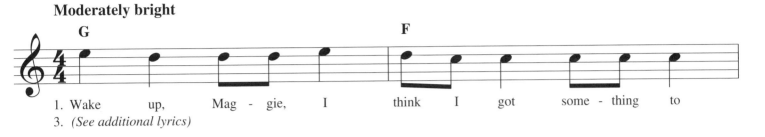

1. Wake up, Mag - gie, I think I got some - thing to
3. *(See additional lyrics)*

say to you. ___ It's late Sep - tem - ber and I

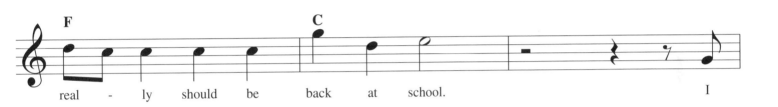

real - ly should be back at school. I

know I keep you a - mused, ___ but I feel I'm be - ing

used, oh, Mag - gie, I could - n't have tried ___ an - y -

more. ___ You led me a - way from

home, just to save you from be - ing a -

148

lone.   You stole my heart___ and that's what real - ly

hurts.   2. The morn - ing sun, when it's

4. *(See additional lyrics)*

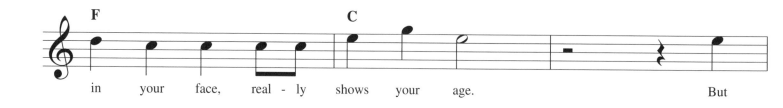

in your face, real - ly shows your age.   But

that don't wor - ry me none in my eyes you're ev - 'ry - thing.

I laughed at all of your

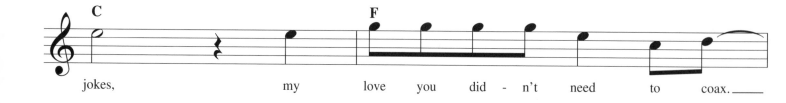

jokes,   my love you did - n't need to coax.___

Oh, Mag - gie, I could - n't have tried _____ an - y -

more. _____ You led me a - way from

home just to save you from bein' a - lone. You

stole my soul, and that's a pain I can do ____ with - out. ____

(Instrumental)

Additional Lyrics

3. All I needed was a friend
   To lend a guiding hand.
   But you turned into a lover, and, mother, what a lover!
   You wore me out.
   All you did was wreck my bed,
   And, in the morning, kick me in the head.
   Oh, Maggie, I couldn't have tried anymore.
   You led me away from home
   'Cause you didn't want to be alone.
   You stole my heart. I couldn't leave you if I tried.

4. I suppose I could collect my books
   And get on back to school.
   Or steal my daddy's cue
   And make a living out of playing pool.
   Or find myself a rock 'n roll band
   That needs a helping hand.
   Oh, Maggie, I wish I'd never seen your face.
   You made a first-class fool out of me.
   But I'm as blind as a fool can be.
   You stole my heart, but I love you anyway.

MISSISSIPPI QUEEN

Words and Music by LESLIE WEST,
FELIX PAPPALARDI, CORKY LAING
and DAVID REA

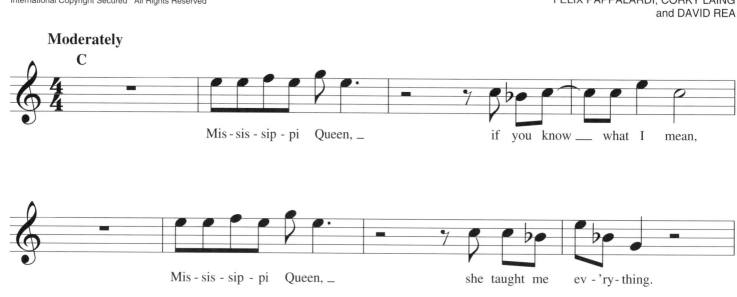

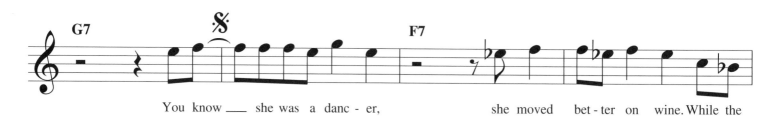

_____ what I mean, Mis - sis - sip - pi Queen, _ she taught me

ev - 'ry - thing. This la - dy, she _ asked me, if I would

be her man. _____ You know _ that I told her I'd do _

_____ what I can to keep _ her look-in' pret-ty, buy her

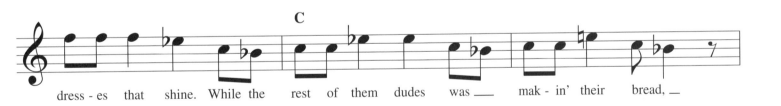

dress - es that shine. While the rest of them dudes was _ mak-in' their bread, _

D.S. al Coda

bud - dy, beg your par - don, I was los - in' mine. You know _

CODA

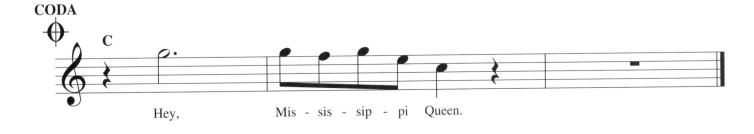

Hey, Mis - sis - sip - pi Queen.

MORE THAN A FEELING

Words and Music by
TOM SCHOLZ

Moderate Rock

I woke up this morn - ing and the sun was gone. ___ I
So man - y peo - ple have come and gone. ___ The

turned up the mu - sic to start my ___ day. ___ I
fac - es ___ fade ___ as the years go ___ by, ___ yet

lost my - self ___ in a fa - mil - iar song. I
I still re - call ___ as I wan - der on, as

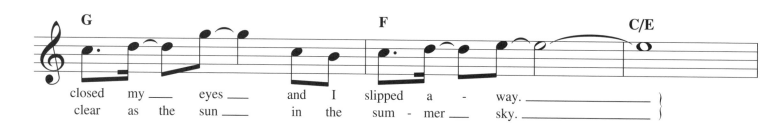

closed my ___ eyes ___ and I slipped a - way. ___
clear as the sun ___ in the sum - mer ___ sky. ___

(Instrumental)

It's more than a feel - ing ___

when I hear that old song ___ they used to play, _____ and

To Coda ⊕

I be - gin dream - ing _____ till I see Mar - i - anne ___ walk ___ a -

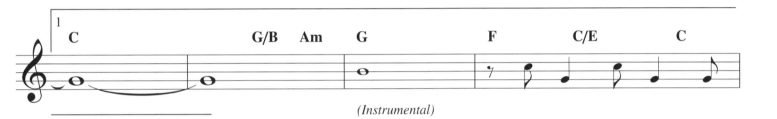

way. I see my Mar - i - anne walk - in' a - way. ___

_____ *(Instrumental)*

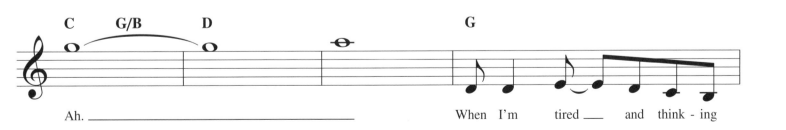

Ah. _____ When I'm tired ___ and think - ing

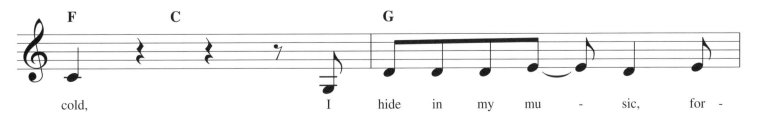

cold, I hide in my mu - sic, for -

get the ____ day ____ and dream of a girl ____ I

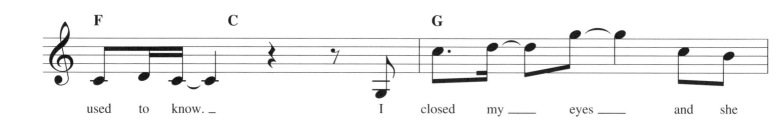

used to know. _ I closed my ____ eyes ____ and she

slipped a - way. ____

She slipped a - way. ____

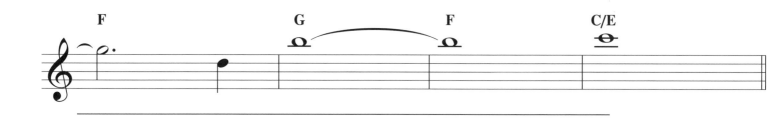

(Instrumental)

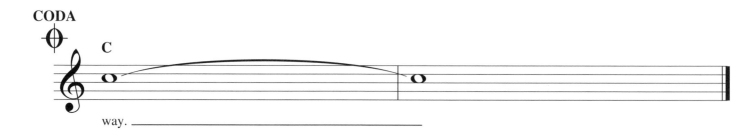

way. ____

Money

Words and Music by
ROGER WATERS

NEW KID IN TOWN

Words and Music by JOHN DAVID SOUTHER,
DON HENLEY and GLENN FREY

158

that it does - n't real - ly mat - ter which side ____

____ you're on. ____ You're walk - ing a - way ____

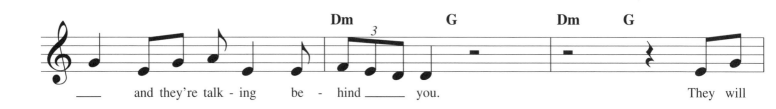

____ and they're talk - ing be - hind ____ you. They will

nev - er for - get you till some - bod - y new comes a - long. ____

Where you been late - ly? There's a new kid in

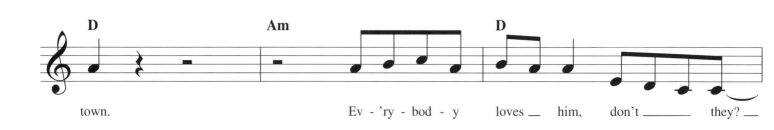

town. Ev - 'ry - bod - y loves ___ him, don't ____ they? ___

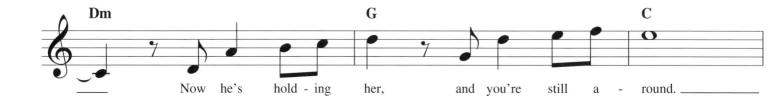

____ Now he's hold - ing her, and you're still a - round. ____

NIGHTS IN WHITE SATIN

Words and Music by
JUSTIN HAYWARD

Moderately

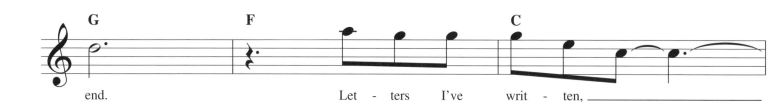

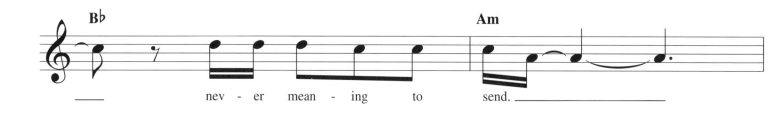

PEACE OF MIND

Words and Music by
TOM SCHOLZ

Moderate Rock

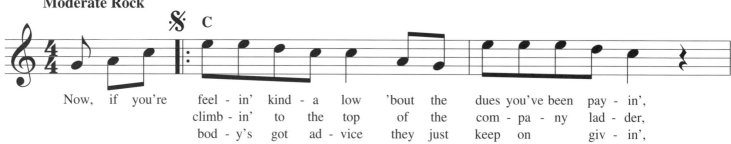

Now, if you're feel-in' kind-a low 'bout the dues you've been pay-in',
climb-in' to the top of the com-pa-ny lad-der,
bod-y's got ad-vice they just keep on giv-in',

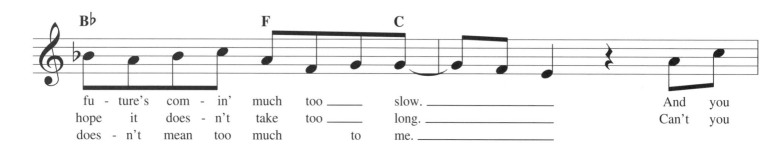

fu-ture's com-in' much too _____ slow. _____ And you
hope it does-n't take too _____ long. _____ Can't you
does-n't mean too much to me. _____

wan-na run but some-how you just keep on stay-in',
see there'll come a day when it won't mat-ter,
Lots of peo-ple have to make be-lieve they're liv-in';

can't de-cide on which way to go. _____ Whoa. _____ Yeah, yeah, yeah.
come a day when you'll be gone. _____ Whoa. _____
can't de-cide who they should be. _____ Whoa. _____

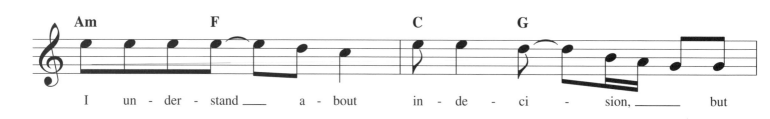

I un-der-stand _____ a-bout in-de-ci-sion, _____ but

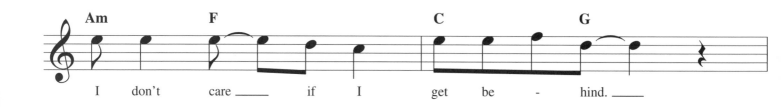

I don't care _____ if I get be-hind. _____

PEG

Words and Music by WALTER BECKER
and DONALD FAGEN

PROUD MARY

Words and Music by
JOHN FOGERTY

Moderately

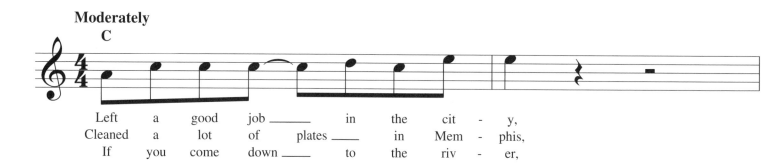

Left a good job ____ in the cit - y,
Cleaned a lot of plates ____ in Mem - phis,
If you come down ____ to the riv - er,

work - in' for the man ____ ev - 'ry night and day. ____
pumped a lot of 'pane ____ down in New Or - leans. ____
bet you gon - na find ____ some ____ peo - ple who live.

And, I nev - er lost ____ one min - ute of sleep - in',
But, I nev - er saw ____ the good ____ side of the cit - y
You don't have to wor - ry ____ 'cause ____ you have no mon - ey.

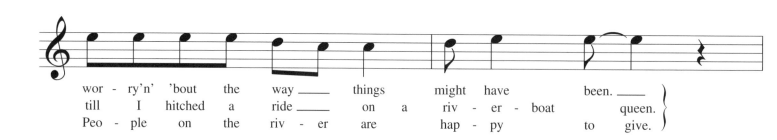

wor - ry'n' 'bout the way ____ things might have been. ____)
till I hitched a ride ____ on a riv - er - boat queen. }
Peo - ple on the riv - er are hap - py to give.)

Big wheel, ____ keep on turn - in',   proud ____

REELING IN THE YEARS

Words and Music by WALTER BECKER
and DONALD FAGEN

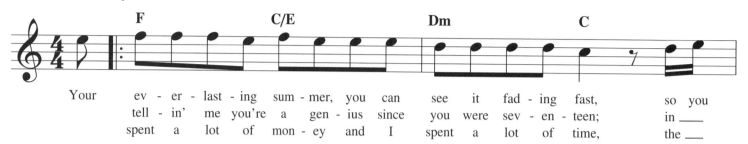

Moderately

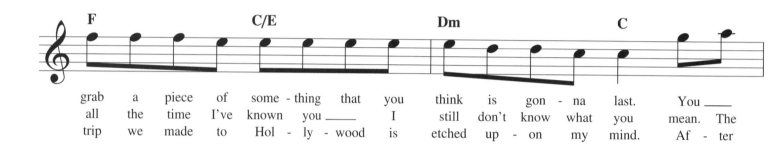

Your ev-er-last-ing sum-mer, you can see it fad-ing fast, so you
tell - in' me you're a gen - ius since you were sev - en - teen; in ___
spent a lot of mon-ey and I spent a lot of time, the ___

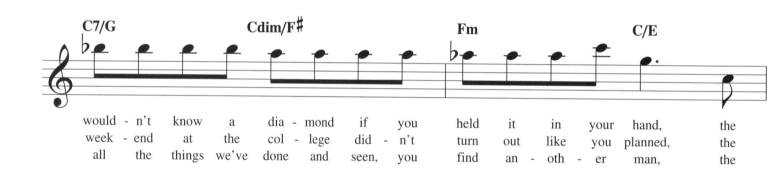

grab a piece of some-thing that you think is gon-na last. You ___
all the time I've known you ___ I still don't know what you mean. The
trip we made to Hol-ly-wood is etched up-on my mind. Af - ter

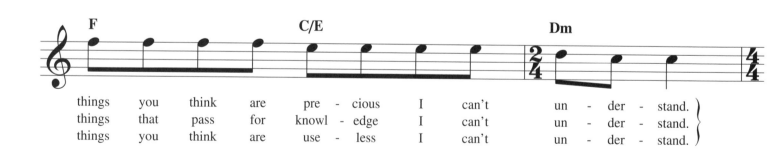

would - n't know a dia-mond if you held it in your hand, the
week - end at the col - lege did - n't turn out like you planned, the
all the things we've done and seen, you find an - oth - er man, the

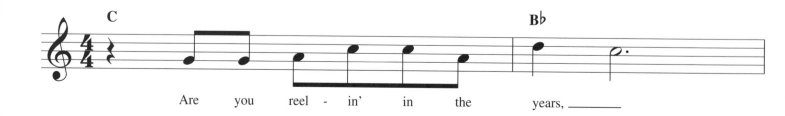

things you think are pre - cious I can't un - der - stand.
things that pass for knowl - edge I can't un - der - stand.
things you think are use - less I can't un - der - stand.

Are you reel - in' in the years, ___

169

stow-in' a - way the time, _____ are you gath-er-in' up the

tears, _____ have you had e - nough of mine? _____

Are you reel - in' in the years, _____ stow - in' a - way the

time, _____ are you gath - er - in' up the

tears, _____ have you had e - nough of

mine? _____

1, 2
3

You been
I

RHIANNON

Words and Music by
STEVIE NICKS

Moderately

Rhi - an - non rings ____ like a bell thru the night, and
She is ____ like a cat in the dark, and

would - n't you love to love ____ her? ____
then she is the dark - ness. ____

Takes to the sky like a bird in flight ____ and
She rules her life like a fine sky - lark ____ and

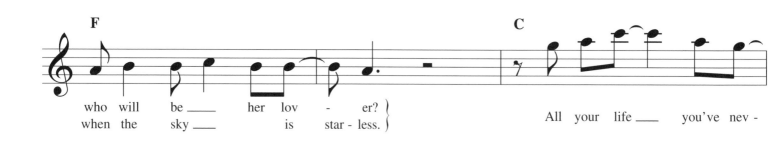

who will be ____ her lov - er?
when the sky ____ is star - less.

All your life ____ you've nev -

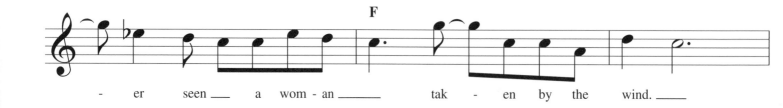

- er seen ____ a wom - an ____ tak - en by the wind. ____

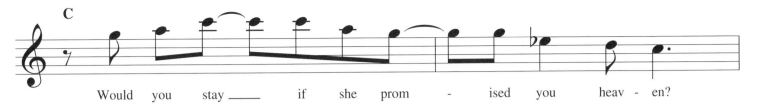

Would you stay ___ if she prom - ised you heav - en?

Will you ev - er win? ___

Will you ev - er win? ___

Am

Play 4 times

F   Am

Rhi - an - non.

Am

Dreams un - wind; love's ___ a state of mind. ___

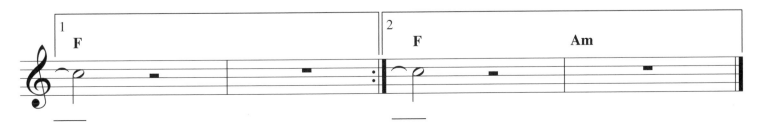

1
F

2
F   Am

RIKKI DON'T LOSE THAT NUMBER

Words and Music by WALTER BECKER
and DONALD FAGEN

ROCK AND ROLL ALL NITE

Words and Music by PAUL STANLEY
and GENE SIMMONS

Moderate Rock

rock and roll ___ all night, _____ and par - ty ev - er - y day.

I wan - na rock and roll ___ all night, _____

and par - ty ev - er - y day. I wan - na rock and roll ___ all night, __

_____ and par - ty ev - er - y day. I wan - na

rock and roll ___ all night, _____ and par - ty ev - er - y day.

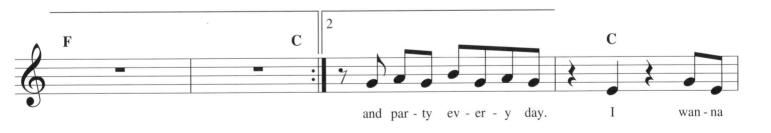

and par - ty ev - er - y day. I wan - na

rock and roll ___ all night, _____ and par - ty ev - er - y day.

R.O.C.K. IN THE U.S.A.
(A Salute to 60's Rock)

Words and Music by
JOHN MELLENCAMP

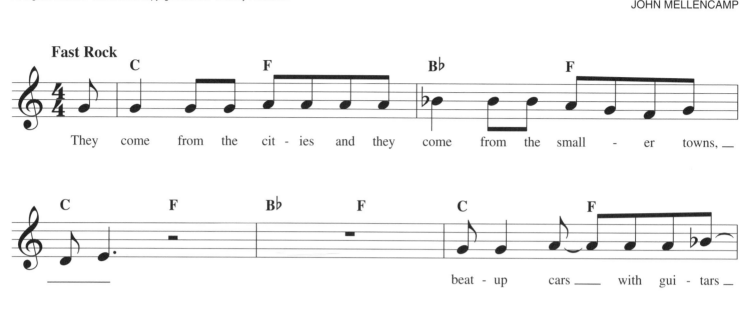

They come from the cit - ies and they come from the small - er towns, _____ beat-up cars ____ with gui - tars _____

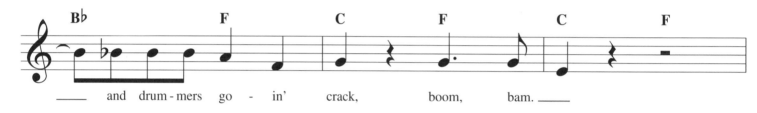

_____ and drum-mers go - in' crack, boom, bam. _____

R. O. C. K. in the U. S. A. ____ R. ____ O. C. K. in the

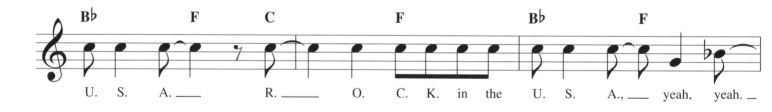

U. S. A. ____ R. ____ O. C. K. in the U. S. A., ____ yeah, yeah. _____

Rock - in' in the U. S. A. _____

Said good - bye ____ to their fam - 'lies, said good-bye to their friends, _____

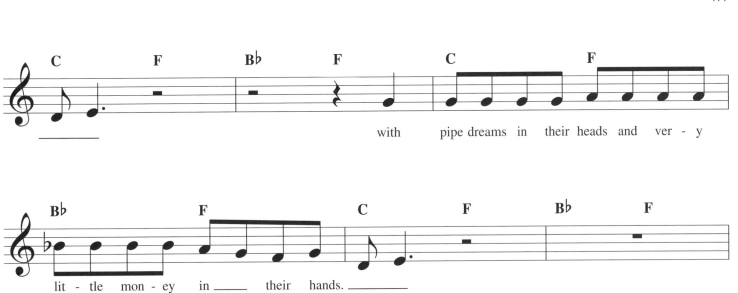

with pipe dreams in their heads and ver - y

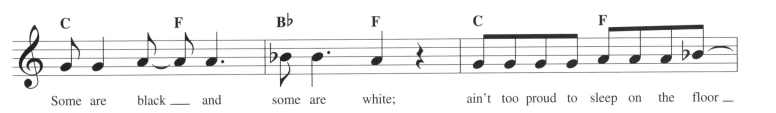

lit - tle mon - ey in ____ their hands. _____

Some are black ___ and some are white; ain't too proud to sleep on the floor __

____ to - night. __ With the blind faith of Je - sus, you know that they ___ just

might be rock - in' in the U. S. A. _____

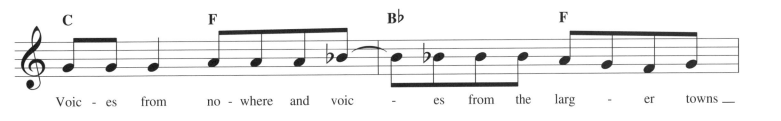

Voic - es from no - where and voic - es from the larg - er towns __

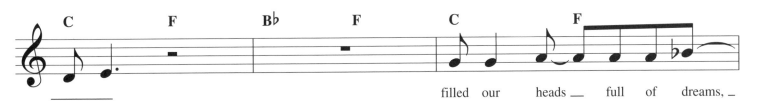

filled our heads __ full of dreams, __

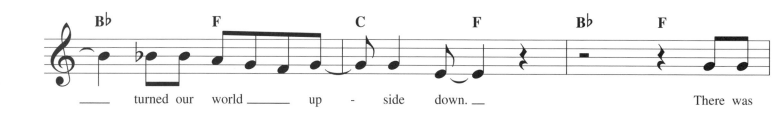

_____ turned our world _____ up - side down. _____ There was

Frank - ie Ly - mon, Bob - by Ful - ler, Mitch Ry - der, (They were rock - in'.)

Jack - ie Wil - son, Shan - gri - Las, Young Ras - cals, (They were rock - in'.)

spot - light on Mar - tha Reeves, _____ let's don't for - get James Brown. _____

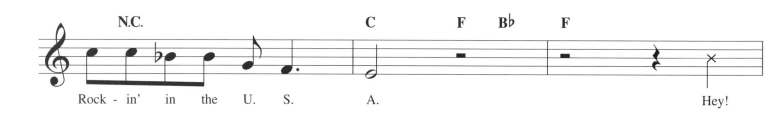

Rock - in' in the U. S. A. Hey!

R. O. C. K. in the U. S. A. _____ R. _____

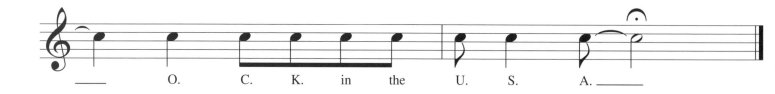

_____ O. C. K. in the U. S. A. _____

NO MATTER WHAT

Written by PETER HAM

Medium Power Rock

No mat - ter what you are, ___ I ___ will al - ways be with

you. Does - n't mat - ter what you do, ___ girl. ___

Ooh, ___ girl, ___ want you. ___ No mat - ter where you

go, ___ I ___ will al - ways be a - round.

Won't you tell me what you found, ___ girl? ___ Ooh, ___ girl, ___ want

180

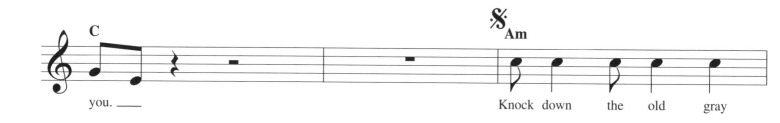

you. ___

Knock down the old gray

wall. Be a part ___ of it all. ___ Noth - ing to

say, noth - ing to see, ___ noth - ing to do. ___

If you would give me all, ___ as

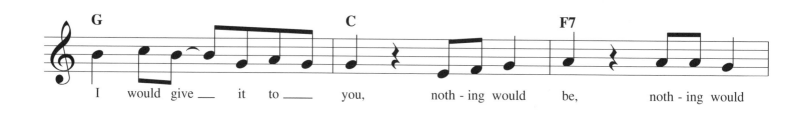

I would give ___ it to ___ you, noth - ing would be, noth - ing would

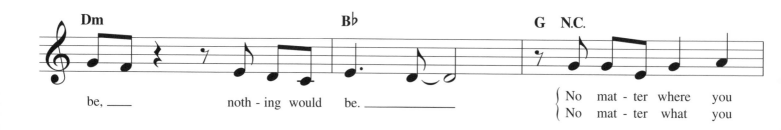

be, ___ noth - ing would be. ___

No mat - ter where you
No mat - ter what you

go, _____   there _____ will al - ways be a
are, _____   I _____ will al - ways be with

place.   Can't you see it in my face, girl? _____
you.   Does - n't mat - ter what you do, girl. _____

To Coda   **D.S. al Coda**

Ooh, _____ girl, _____ want you. _____

CODA

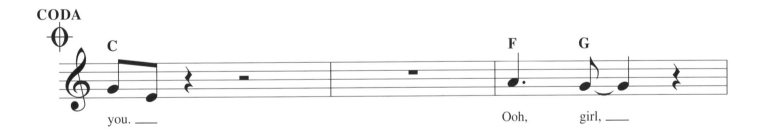

you. _____   Ooh, girl, _____

you, _____ girl, _____ want you. _____

Ooh, girl, _____ you, _____ girl, _____ want you. _____

ROCK'N ME

Words and Music by
STEVE MILLER

Moderately

Well, I been look - in' real hard and I'm try'n' to find a job, but it
Don't get sus - pi - cious, now don't be sus - pi - cious. Babe, you

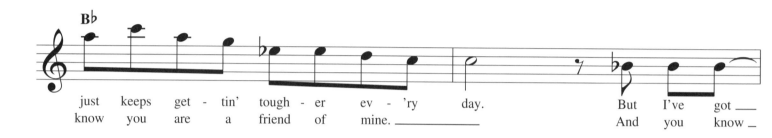

just keeps get - tin' tough - er ev - 'ry day. But I've got ___
know you are a friend of mine. ___ And you know ___

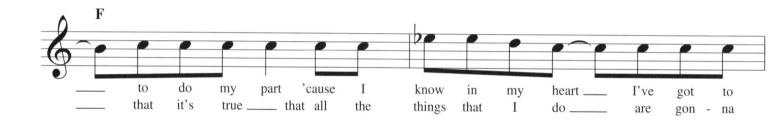

___ to do my part 'cause I know in my heart ___ I've got to
___ that it's true ___ that all the things that I do ___ are gon - na

please my sweet ba - by, yeah. ___ Well, I ain't ___
come back to you in your sweet time. ___ I went from

___ su - per - sti - tious and I don't get sus - pi - cious, 'cause my
Phoe - nix, Ar - i - zo - na, all the way to Ta - co - ma, Phil - a -

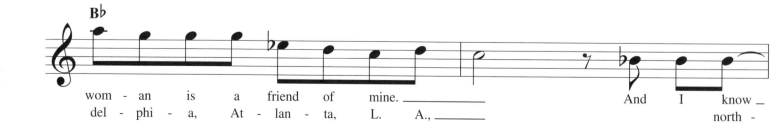

wom - an is a friend of mine. ___ And I know ___
del - phi - a, At - lan - ta, L. A., ___ north -

F

that it's true ___ that all the things that I do ___ will come back ___
-ern Cal - i - for - nia where the girls are warm ___ so I could

C   **To Coda** ⊕

to me in my sweet time. _____ So keep on
be with my sweet ba - by, yeah. _____ Keep on a -
hear my sweet ba - by say: _____ Keep on a -

B♭

rock - in' me, ba - by;   keep on a - rock - in' me, ba - by;

F

keep on a - rock - in' me, ba - by;   keep on a -

C

rock - in' me, ba - by.   I went from

1.   2.
Ba - by, ba - by, ba - by, keep on

F   **C**   **F**

rock - in',   rock - in' me, ba - by.

Keep on a - rock - in', rock - in' me, ba - by.

(Instrumental) D.S. al Coda

CODA

rock - in' me, ba - by; keep on a -

rock - in' me, ba - by; keep on a - rock - in' me, ba - by;

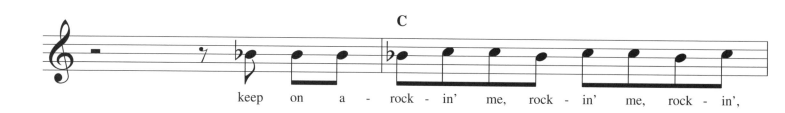

keep on a - rock - in' me, rock - in' me, rock - in',

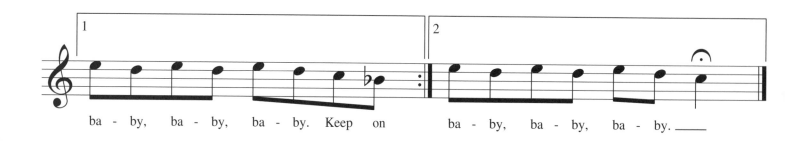

ba - by, ba - by, ba - by. Keep on   ba - by, ba - by, ba - by. _____

ROCKY MOUNTAIN WAY

Words and Music by JOE WALSH, JOE VITALE,
KEN PASSARELLI and ROCKE GRACE

Moderately

Spent the last ____ year Rock - y Moun - tain Way, _____
tell - in' us this and he's tell - in' us that, chang - es it ev - 'ry day; _____

could - n't get much high - er. ____   Out to pas - ture,
says it does - n't mat - ter. ____   Bas - es are load - ed and Cas - ey's at bat,

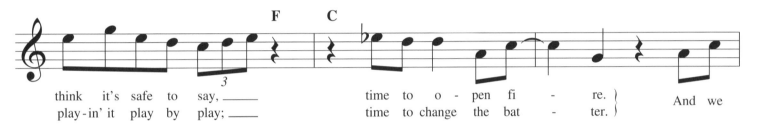

think it's safe to say, _____   time to o - pen fi - re.)   And we
play - in' it play by play; _____   time to change the bat - ter.)

don't need the la - dies cry - in' 'cause the sto - ry's sad, ____   'cause the

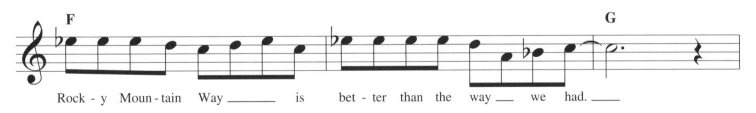

Rock - y Moun - tain Way _____ is bet - ter than the way ___ we had.

Whoa. _____   Ooh, _ hoo. _   *(Instrumental)*

Well, he's _____   *(Instrumental)*

SHOW ME THE WAY

Words and Music by
PETER FRAMPTON

Moderately

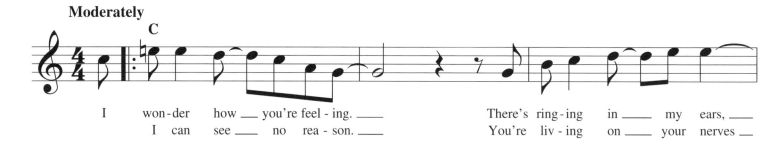

I won-der how __ you're feel-ing. _____ There's ring-ing in ____ my ears, ____
I can see __ no rea-son. _____ You're liv-ing on ____ your nerves __

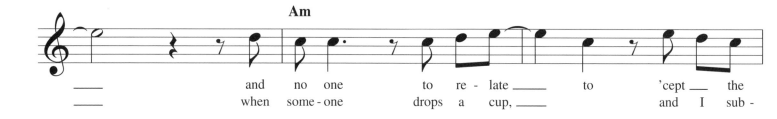

___ and no one to re-late ____ to 'cept __ the
___ when some-one drops a cup, ___ and I sub-

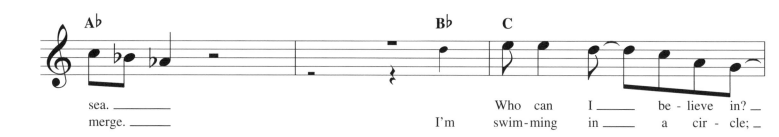

sea. _____ Who can I ____ be-lieve in?
merge. _____ I'm swim-ming in ____ a cir-cle; _

I'm kneel-ing on ____ the floor. _____ There
I feel I'm go-ing down. _____ There

has to be ____ a force; who do _____ I phone? _
has to be ____ a fool to play ____ my part. __

pen - ing _____ to me. _____ I watch you when _ you're sleep -

ing; well, then I _____ want to take _ your love. _____ Oh, won't

you _____ show me the way, ev - 'ry day? _

_____ I want you; _____ show me the

way. One more time! _____ I want you _____ day af - ter

day. _____ Yeah, I want you _____ day af - ter

day, _____ hey, _____ hey. _____

SAME OLD SONG AND DANCE

Words and Music by STEVEN TYLER
and JOE PERRY

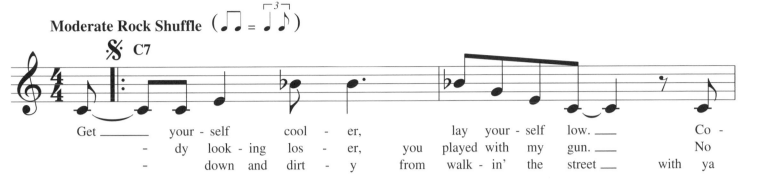

Moderate Rock Shuffle

Get _____ your - self cool - er, lay your - self low. _____ Co -
- dy look - ing los - er, you played with my gun. _____ No
- down and dirt - y from walk - in' the street _____ with ya

in - ci - den - tal mur - der with noth - in' to show, _____ when the judge -
smooth - faced law - yer to get - cha un - done. _____ Say love _____
old hur - dy - gur - dy and no one to meet, _____ say love _____

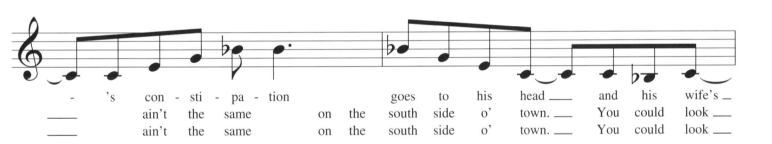

- 's con - sti - pa - tion goes to his head _____ and his wife's _____
_____ ain't the same on the south side o' town. _____ You could look _____
_____ ain't the same on the south side o' town. _____ You could look _____

_____ ag - gra - va - tion you're soon e - nough dead. _____
_____ but you ain't gon - na find it a - round. _____ } It's the same _____
_____ but you ain't gon - na find it a - round. _____

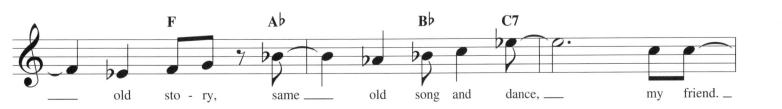

_____ old sto - ry, same _____ old song and dance, _____ my friend. _____

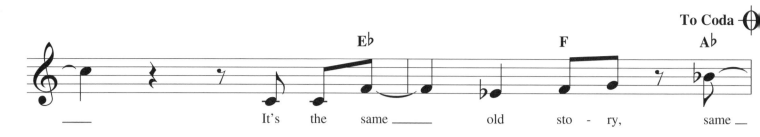

It's the same ___ old sto - ry, same ___

___ old song and dance, ___ my friend. ___ Sha -

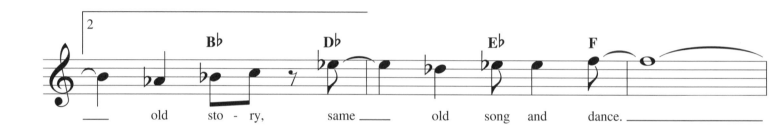

___ old sto - ry, same ___ old song and dance. ___

___ (Instrumental) Fate ___

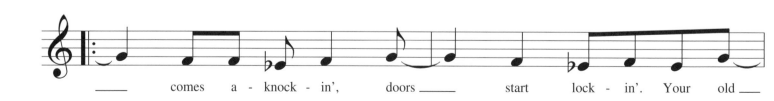

___ comes a - knock - in', doors ___ start lock - in'. Your old ___

___ time con - nec - tion, change ___ of di - rec - tion. You ain't

gon - na change it, can't _____ re - ar - range it, can't _____

_____ stand the pain when it's all _____ the same _____ to you, _____

_____ my friend. _____ Fate _____

(Instrumental) When you're low -

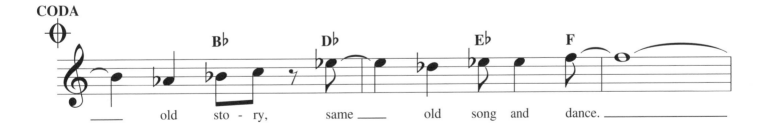

_____ old sto - ry, same _____ old song and dance. _____

(Instrumental)

Slow Ride

Words and Music by
LONESOME DAVE PEVERETT

Moderate Rock beat

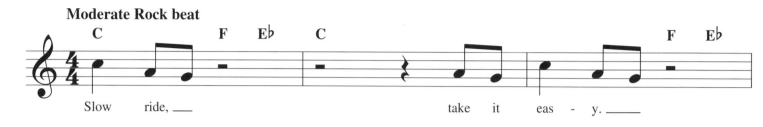

Slow ride, ___ take it eas - y. ___

Slow ride, ___ take it

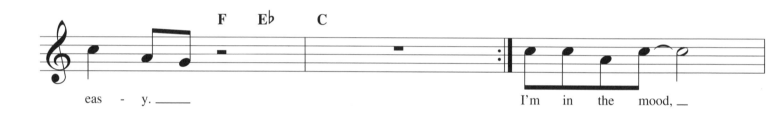

eas - y. ___ I'm in the mood, __

the rhy - thm is right. __

Move to the mu - sic, we can roll all night. __

(Instrumental) Slow ___ ride. (Instrumental)

Slow ride, ___ take it

eas - y. ___ Slow ride, ___ take it

eas - y. ___ Slow down, go down.

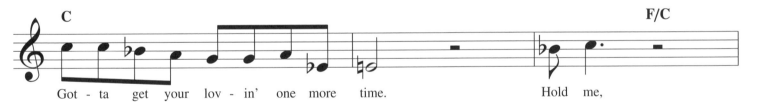

Got - ta get your lov - in' one more time. Hold me,

roll me. Slow - rid - in' wom - an, you're so ___ fine. ___

Repeat and Fade

Slow ride, ___ eas - y. ___

SMALL TOWN

Words and Music by
JOHN MELLENCAMP

Moderately fast

Well,   I   was   born   in   a   small _____ town,
Ed - u - cat - ed   in _____ a   small _____ town,

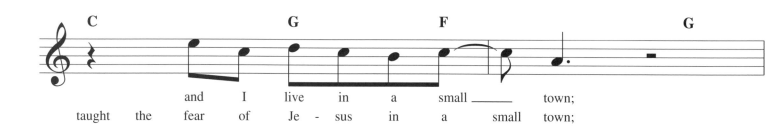

and   I   live   in   a   small _____ town;
taught   the   fear   of   Je - sus   in   a   small   town;

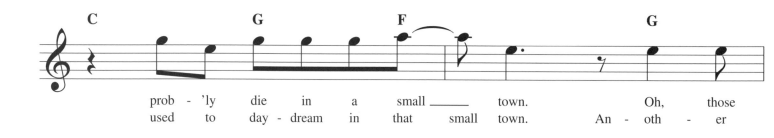

prob - 'ly   die   in   a   small _____ town.   Oh,   those
used   to   day - dream   in   that   small   town.   An - oth - er

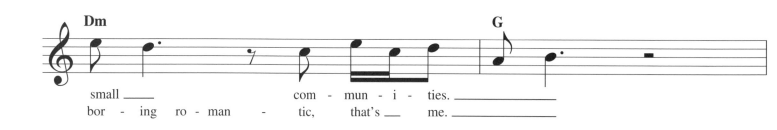

small _____ com - mun - i - ties. _____
bor - ing   ro - man - tic,   that's __ me. _____

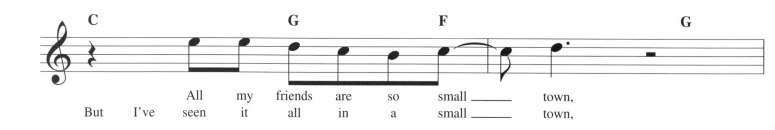

All   my   friends   are   so   small _____ town,
But   I've   seen   it   all   in   a   small _____ town,

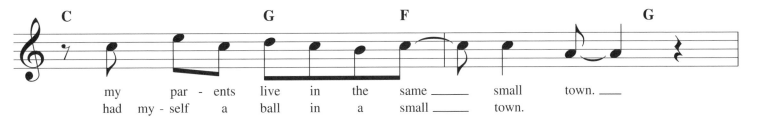

my par - ents live in the same _____ small town. _____
had my - self a ball in a small _____ town. _____

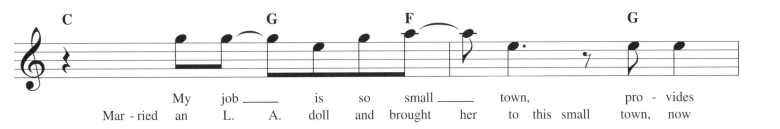

My job _____ is so small _____ town, pro - vides
Mar - ried an L. A. doll and brought her to this small town, now

lit - tle op - por - tu - ni - ties. _____
she's small town _ just like _____ me. _

No, I can - not for - get _____ where it is _____ that I _____ come from, I

can - not for - get the peo - ple who love _____ me. Yeah, I can be my - self _____ here in

this small town, _ and peo - ple let _____ me be _____ just what I want to be.

Got noth-ing a-gainst a big _____ town,

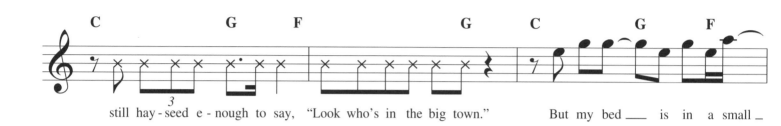

still hay-seed e-nough to say, "Look who's in the big town." But my bed ___ is in a small ___

___ town; oh, and that's good e - nough __ for me. _____

Well, I was born in a small ___ town, and I can breathe in a small __

___ town. Gon - na die ___ in this small ___ town, and that's

prob - 'ly where they'll bur - y me. _____

SOMEBODY TO LOVE

Words and Music by
DARBY SLICK

Moderately fast

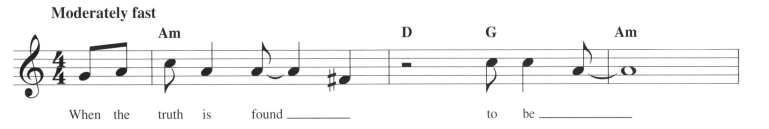

When the truth is found _____ to be _____

lies, and all of the joy _____ with - in you _____

____ dies, don't you want some - bod - y to love? _

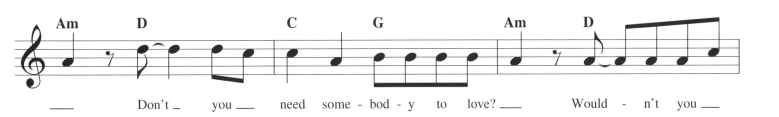

____ Don't _ you ____ need some - bod - y to love? ____ Would - n't you ____

love some - bod - y to love? ____ You ____ bet - ter find ____ some - bod - y to love. ____

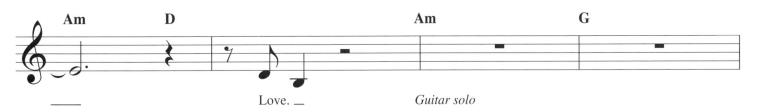

____ Love. ____ *Guitar solo*

SMOKE ON THE WATER

Words and Music by RITCHIE BLACKMORE, IAN GILLAN,
ROGER GLOVER, JON LORD and IAN PAICE

Moderate Rock

We all came out to Mon - treux on the
They burned down the gam - bling house, it
We end - ed up at the Grand Ho - tel,

Lake Ge - ne - va shore - line
died with an aw - ful sound.
it was emp - ty, cold and bare. But with the

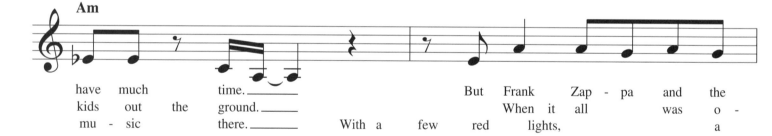

to make rec - ords with the mo - bile, we did - n't
A funk - y Claude was run-ning in and out, pull - ing
Roll - in' Truck Stones thing just out - side, mak - ing our

have much time. But Frank Zap - pa and the
kids out the ground. When it all was o -
mu - sic there. With a few red lights, a

Moth - ers were at the best place a - round.
- ver, we had to find an - oth - er place.
few old beds, we made a place to sweat.

Am

— But some stu - pid with a flare gun
— But Swiss time was run - ning out, it
— No mat - ter what we get out of this,

STILL THE SAME

Words and Music by
BOB SEGER

Moderately, with a beat

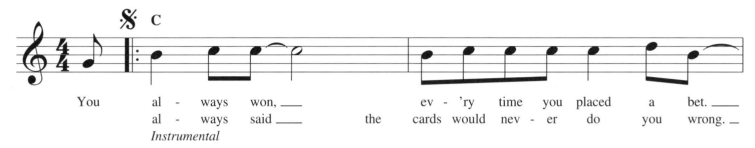

You al - ways won, ___ ev - 'ry time you placed a bet. ___
al - ways said ___ the cards would nev - er do you wrong. ___
Instrumental

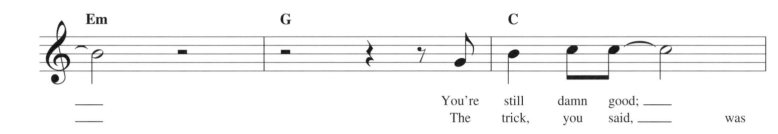

___ You're still damn good; ___
___ The trick, you said, ___ was

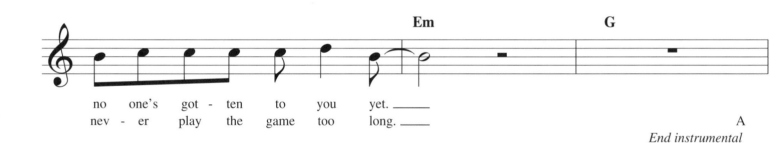

no one's got - ten to you yet. _____
nev - er play the game too long. ___
End instrumental

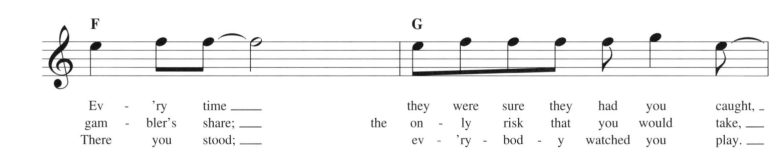

Ev - 'ry time ___ they were sure they had you caught, _
gam - bler's share; ___ the on - ly risk that you would take, ___
There you stood; ___ ev - 'ry - bod - y watched you play. __

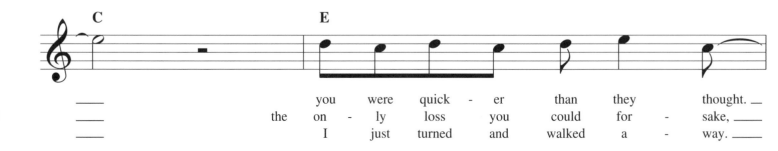

___ you were quick - er than they thought. ___
___ the on - ly loss you could for - sake, ___
___ I just turned and walked a - way. ___

Am · **Dm** · **G** · **To Coda** ⊕

You'd just turn your back and walk. ___
the on - ly bluff you could - n't fake. ___
I had noth - ing left to say. ___

1 · **2** · **C**

You

And you're still the same. ___

I

E · **A**

caught up with you yes - ter - day. _____

Mov - in' game to game; ___

Dm · **G**

___

no one stand - in' in your way. ___

C · **E**

Turn - in' on the charm ___

long e - nough to get you by. ___

204

You're still the same. ____

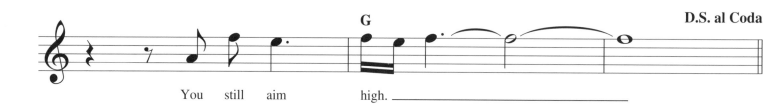
You still aim high. ____

D.S. al Coda

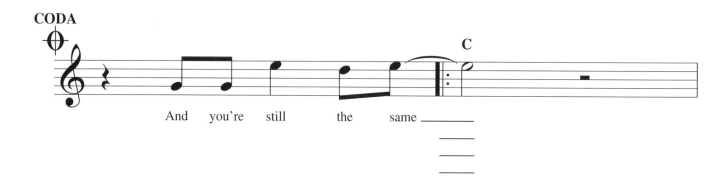
CODA
And you're still the same ____

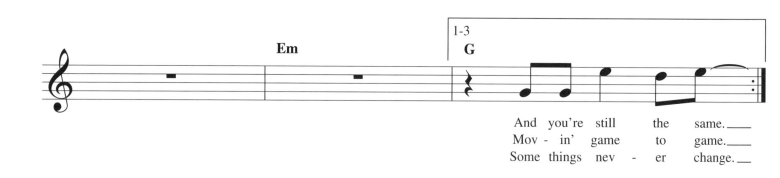
1-3
And you're still the same. ____
Mov - in' game to game. ____
Some things nev - er change. __

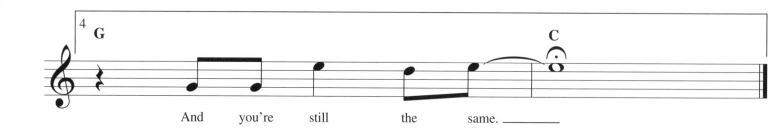
4
And you're still the same. ____

Sunshine of Your Love

Words and Music by JACK BRUCE,
PETE BROWN and ERIC CLAPTON

Moderate Rock

It's get - ting near dawn _____ when
with you my love; _____ the

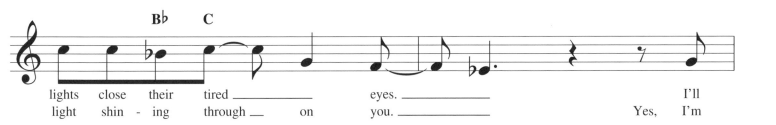

lights close their tired _____ eyes. _____ I'll
light shin - ing through _ on you. _____ Yes, I'm

soon be with you, _____ my _____ love, _____ to
with you, my love. _____ It's the

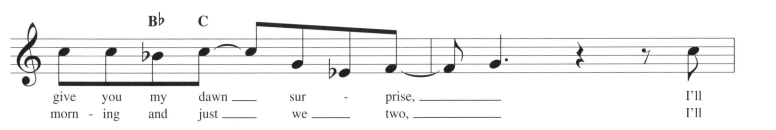

give you my dawn _____ sur - prise, _____ I'll
morn - ing and just _____ we _____ two, _____ I'll

be with you, dar - ling soon. _____ I'll
stay with you, dar - ling, now. _____ I'll

To Coda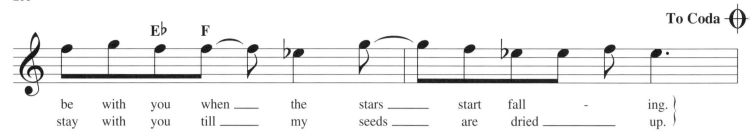

be with you when ____ the stars ____ start fall - ing.
stay with you till ____ my seeds ____ are dried ____ up.

(Instrumental)

I've ____ been wait - ing so ____ long

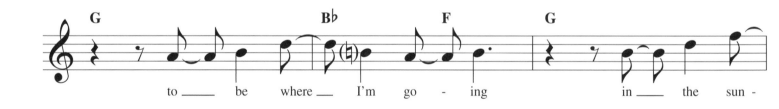

to ____ be where ____ I'm go - ing in ____ the sun -

- shine of ____ your love. ____

D.S. al Coda

(Instrumental)

I'm

CODA

(Instrumental)

I've ___ been wait -

- ing so ___ long. I've ___ been wait - ing ___ so long. ___

I've ___ been wait - ing so ___ long to ___ be where ___

___ I'm go - ing in ___ the sun - shine of ___ your

love. ___

SULTANS OF SWING

Words and Music by
MARK KNOPFLER

Medium bright Rock

1. You get a shiv-er in the dark, it's ___ rain-ing in the park, but mean-
2. step in - side but you don't see too man-y fac-
3.-6. *(See additional lyrics)*

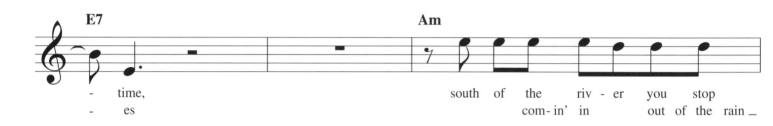

- time,
- es

south of the riv-er you stop

com-in' in out of the rain ___

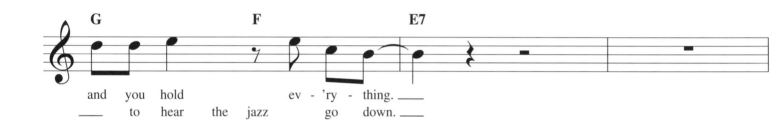

and you hold ev - 'ry - thing. ___
___ to hear the jazz go down. ___

A band is blow-in' Dix - ie dou-ble four ___ time.
Com-pe - ti-tion, too man - y oth-er plac-es,

You feel all right when you hear the mu - sic ring. ___
but the horns, they're blow - in' that

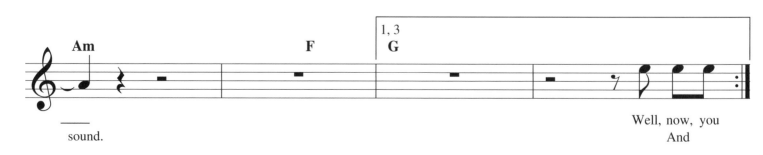

1, 3

___
sound.

Well, now, you
And

Way on down ___ south, way on down south

Lon-don Town. ___ *(Instrumental)*

To Coda ⊕

D.S. for additional verses
(After last verse, To Coda)

3. You check out

CODA ⊕

Additional Lyrics

3. You check out Guitar George, he knows all them fancy chords.
He's just rhythm, gonna make that guitar cry and make it sing
This and an old guitar is just all he can afford,
When he gets up under the coloured lights, gonna play his thing.

4. And Harry doesn't mind if he doesn't make that fancy scene.
He's got a daytime job, he's doin' quite all right, thank you very much.
He can do the honky-tonk just like anything,
Savin' it up for Friday night
With the Sultans, with the Sultans Of Swing.

5. And a crowd of young boys, they're just foolin' around in the corner,
Drunk and dressed in their baggies and their best King's Road.
They don't give a damn about any trumpet playin' band;
It ain't what they call rock and roll.
And the Sultans, yeah the Sultans, they played Creole.

6. And then The Man, he steps right up to the microphone
And says, at last, just as the time-bell rings:
"Thank you, good night, now it's time to go home."
And he makes it fast with one more thing:
"We are the Sultans, we are the Sultans Of Swing."
To Coda

SUMMER IN THE CITY

Words and Music by JOHN SEBASTIAN,
STEVE BOONE and MARK SEBASTIAN

Hot town, sum-mer in the cit-y,
Cool town, eve-nin' in the cit-y,

back o' my neck get-tin' dirt-y and grit-ty.
dressed up so fine and a-look-in' so pret-ty.

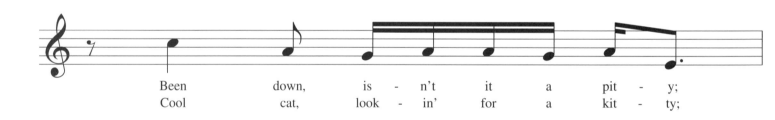

Been down, is-n't it a pit-y;
Cool cat, look-in' for a kit-ty;

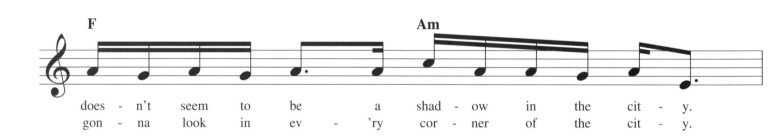

does-n't seem to be a shad-ow in the cit-y.
gon-na look in ev-'ry cor-ner of the cit-y.

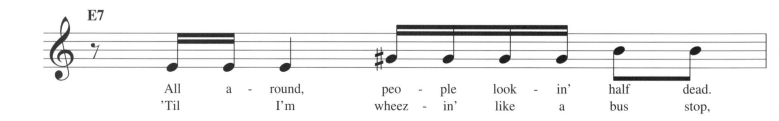

All a-round, peo-ple look-in' half dead.
'Til I'm wheez-in' like a bus stop,

Walk - in' on the side - walk hot - ter than a match, yeah, _____
run - nin' up the stairs gonna meet you on the roof - top. _____

_____ } But at night it's a dif - f'rent world; _

go out and find a girl. _ Come on, come on and dance _ all night; _

de - spite the heat it - 'll be al - right. _ And babe, don't you know it's a pit - y, the

days can't be like the nights in the sum - mer _____ in the cit - y, _____ in the

1
sum - mer _____ in the cit - y. _____
2
sum - mer _____ in the cit - y. _____

SWEET EMOTION

Words and Music by STEVEN TYLER
and TOM HAMILTON

Moderately

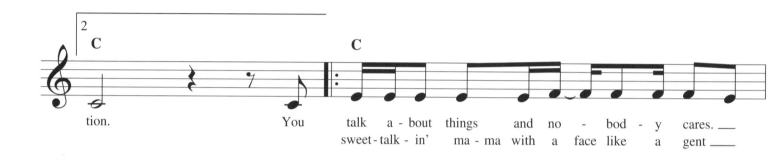

Sweet _____ e - mo - tion.

tion.   You   talk a - bout things   and no - bod - y   cares. ___
                          sweet - talk - in'   ma - ma with a   face like   a   gent ___

You're   wear - in' out   things   that no - bod - y   wears. ___
said   my   get - up - and - go   must have got   up   and went. ___

You're   call - in' my   name   but I   got - ta make   clear, ___
Well,   I   got   good   news, she's a   real   good li - ar

I   can't say, ba - by, where I'll be in a year. _____
'cause my   back - stage boo - gie set yo' pants _ on ___ fire. ___

Some

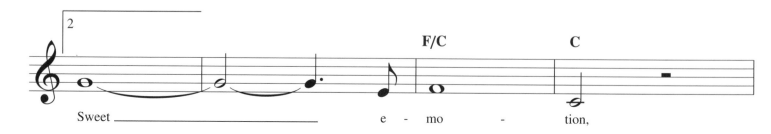

Sweet _____ e - mo - tion,

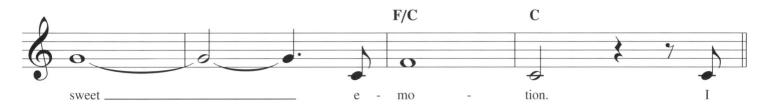

sweet _____ e - mo - tion. I

pulled in - to town in a po - lice car; ___ your
Stand in front just a - shak - in' your ass; I'll

dad - dy said I took you just a lit - tle too far. You're
take you back - stage, you can drink from my glass. I'm

tell - in' her things but your girl - friend lied; you
talk - in' 'bout some - thin' you can sure un - der - stand, 'cause a

can't catch me 'cause the rab - bit done died.
month on the road and I'll be eat - in' from your hand.

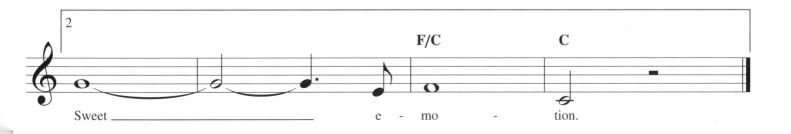

Sweet _____ e - mo - tion.

SWEET HOME ALABAMA

Words and Music by RONNIE VAN ZANT,
ED KING and GARY ROSSINGTON

Moderately slow

Big wheels keep on turn - ing   car - ry me home to see my

kin.   Sing - ing songs a - bout the South - land

I miss ole 'Bam - y once a - gain.____   *(And I think it's a sin.)*

Well, I heard Mis - ter Young sing a - bout her.

Well, I heard ole Neil___ put her down.   Well, I hope Neil Young will re -

mem - ber   a South - ern man don't need him a - round an - y - how.___

Sweet home Al - a - bam - a,   where the skies are so

blue, sweet home Al - a - bam - a,

Lord, I'm com - ing home to you.

3. In Bir - ming - ham they love the
4. *(See additional lyrics)*

Gov' - nor. Boo! boo! boo! Now we all did what we could do.____

Now Wa - ter - gate does not both - er me. Does your con - science both - er

Chorus

you? *(Tell the truth.)* Sweet home Al - a - bam - a,

where the skies are so blue, sweet home Al - a -

bam - a, Lord, I'm com - ing home to you.

Additional Lyrics

4. Now Muscle Shoals has got the Swampers
And they've been known to pick a tune or two
Lord, they get me off so much
They pick me up when I'm feeling blue
Now how about you.
Chorus

SWEET TALKIN' WOMAN

Words and Music by
JEFF LYNNE

Moderately

Sweet talk - in' wom - an, where did you go? _____ *(Instrumental)*

I was search - in' on a one - way street, _ I was
walk - in', man - y days go by. _____ I was
liv - in' on a dead - end street, _ I've been

hop - in' for a chance to meet. _ I was wait - in' for the op - er - a -
think - in' 'bout the lone - ly nights. _ Com - mun - i - ca - tion break -
ask - in' ev - 'ry - bod - y I meet. In - suf - fi - cient da

- tor on the line. _____
- down all a - round. __   (She's _ gone so long.) What can I do?
- ta com - ing through. _

_____ (Where could she be?)   Don't know what I'm gon - na do, _

_____ I got - ta get back _ to you. _____

(You got - ta.) Slow down, sweet talk - in' wom - an.

You got me run-nin', you got me search - in'. Hold on,

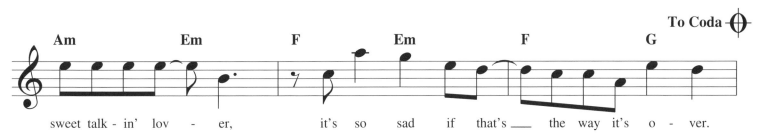

sweet talk - in' lov - er, it's so sad if that's ___ the way it's o - ver.

(Instrumental) I was I've been

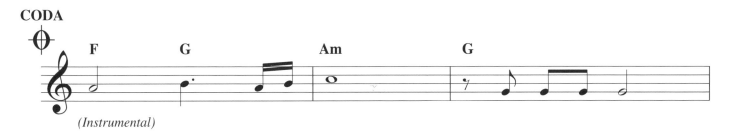

(Instrumental)

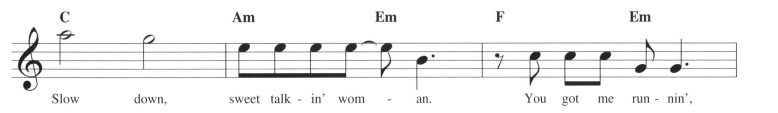

Slow down, sweet talk - in' wom - an. You got me run - nin',

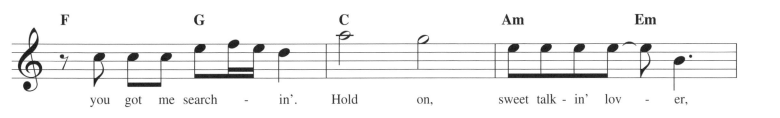

you got me search - in'. Hold on, sweet talk - in' lov - er,

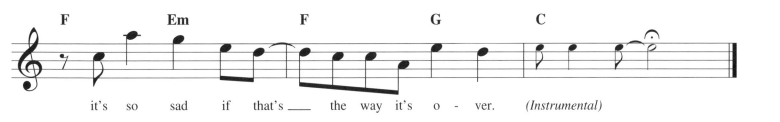

it's so sad if that's ___ the way it's o - ver. (Instrumental)

TAKIN' CARE OF BUSINESS

Words and Music by
RANDY BACHMAN

Moderate Rock

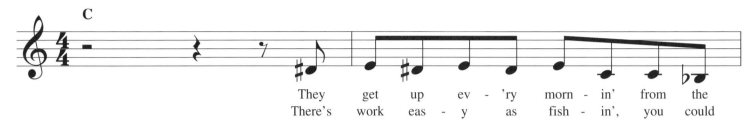

They get up ev-'ry morn-in' from the
There's work eas-y as fish-in', you could

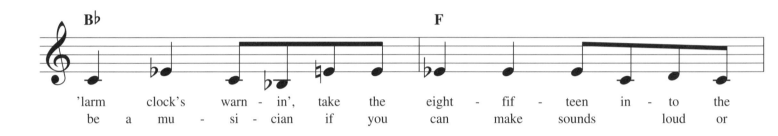

'larm clock's warn-in', take the eight-fif-teen in-to the
be a mu-si-cian if you can make sounds loud or

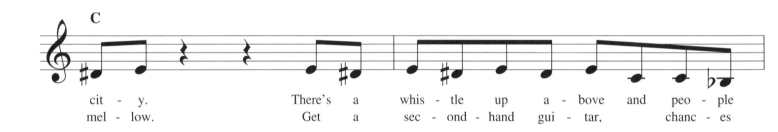

cit-y. There's a whis-tle up a-bove and peo-ple
mel-low. Get a sec-ond-hand gui-tar, chanc-es

push-in', peo-ple shov-in' and the girls who try to look
are you'll go far if you get in with the right bunch of

pret-ty. And if your train's on time, you can
fel-lows. Peo-ple see you hav-in' fun just a

get to work by nine and start your slav-in' job to get your
ly-in' in the sun. Tell them that you like it this

pay.   If   you   ev - er   get   an - noyed,   look   at
way.   It's   the   work that we   a - void   and   we're

me: I'm self - em - ployed.   I   love   to   work   at   noth - in'   all
all   self - em - ployed.   We   love   to   work   at   noth - in'   all

day.   And I've been   tak - in' care   of   bus' - ness,
day.   And we   been

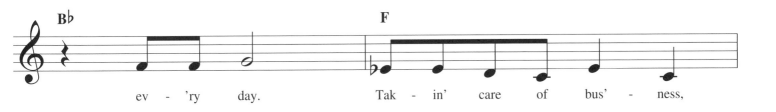

ev - 'ry   day.   Tak - in' care   of   bus' - ness,

ev - 'ry   way.   I've been tak - in' care   of   bus' - ness,

it's   all   mine.   Tak - in' care   of   bus' - ness and

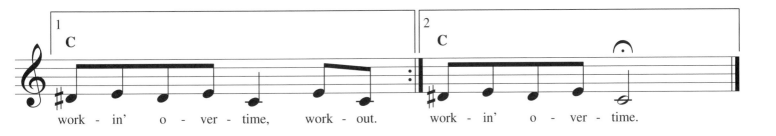

1
work - in' o - ver - time,   work - out.

2
work - in' o - ver - time.

TAKIN' IT TO THE STREETS

Words and Music by
MICHAEL McDONALD

Moderately fast

You don't know ___ me, but I'm your ___ broth - er. ___
Take this mes - sage ___ to my ___ broth - er. ___

___ I was raised ___ here in ___ this
___ You will find ___ him ev - 'ry -

liv - ing ___ hell. ___ You don't know _
where, wher - ev - er peo -

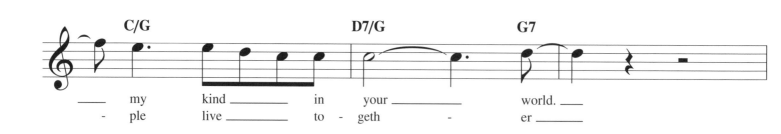

___ my kind ___ in your ___ world. ___
- ple live ___ to - geth - er ___

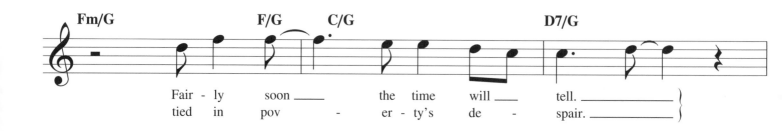

Fair - ly soon ___ the time will ___ tell. ___
tied in pov - er - ty's de - spair. ___

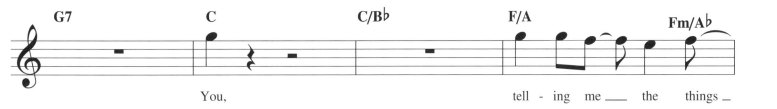

You,

tell - ing me ___ the things ___

___ you're gon - na do for me. ___

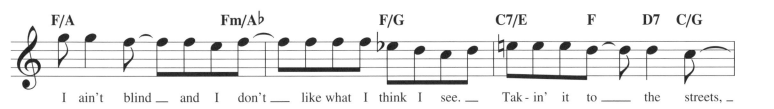

I ain't blind ___ and I don't ___ like what I think I see. ___ Tak - in' it to ___ the streets, ___

___ tak - in' it to ___ the streets, ___

tak - in' it to ___ the streets, ___ tak - in' it to ___ the streets. ___

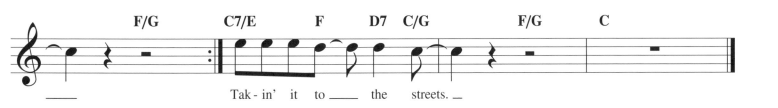

___ Tak - in' it to ___ the streets. ___

THAT'S ALL

Words and Music by TONY BANKS,
PHIL COLLINS and MIKE RUTHERFORD

Just as I thought — it was go-ing al - right, I found out I'm wrong —

—— when I thought I was right. It's al-ways the same, —— it's just a shame, that's all. ——

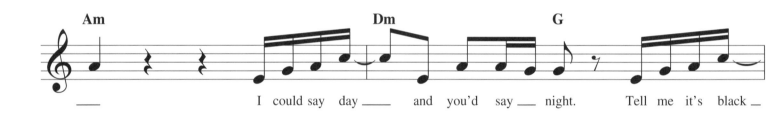

—— I could say day —— and you'd say —— night. Tell me it's black ——

—— when I know that it's white. Al-ways the same, —— it's just a shame, and that's all.

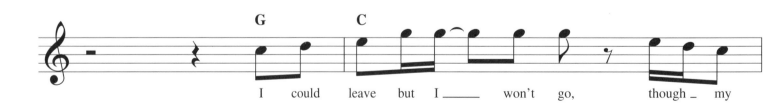

I could leave but I —— won't go, though —— my

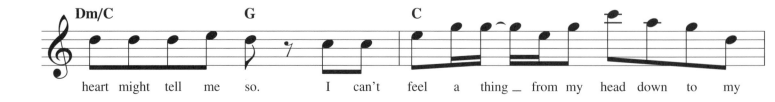

heart might tell me so.   I can't feel a thing —— from my head down to my

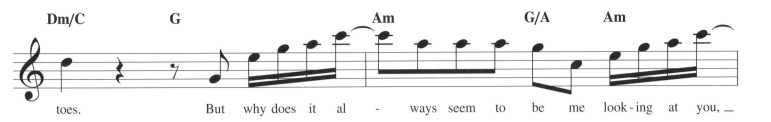

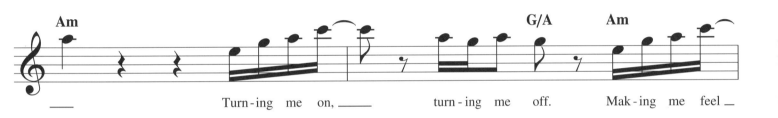

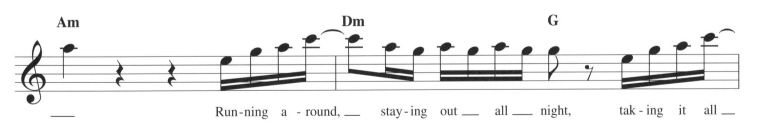

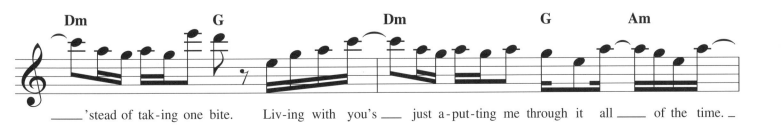

But I could leave, but I ___ won't _ go. Well, it - 'd be

eas - i - er, ___ I ___ know. I can't feel a thing ___ from my head down ___ to my

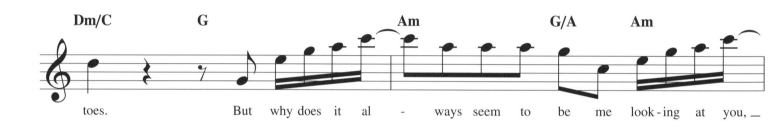

toes. But why does it al - ways seem to be me look - ing at you, _

___ you _ look - ing at ___ me? It's al - ways the same, ___ it's just a shame, that's all. _

___ Truth is I love you ___ more than I want - ed ___ to.

There's no point in try - ing to pre - tend. _____ There's been no one __ who

To Coda ⊕

makes me feel like you do. _____ Say we'll be to - geth - er

D.S. al Coda

Am   **G**

CODA ⊕

Am

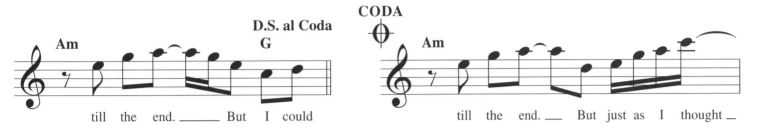

till the end. _____ But I could   till the end. ___ But just as I thought ___

G/A

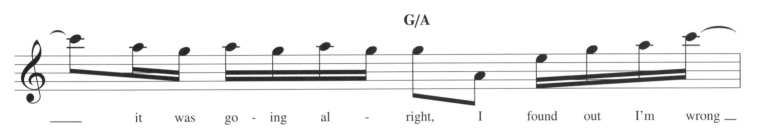

_____ it was go - ing al - right, I found out I'm wrong ___

Am   **G/A**   **Am**   **F**   **G**

_____ when I thought I was right. It's al - ways the same, ___ it's just a shame, that's all. ___

Am   **Dm**   **G**

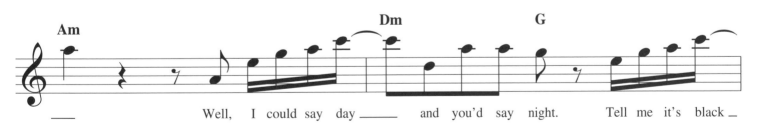

___ Well, I could say day _____ and you'd say night. Tell me it's black ___

Dm   **G**   **Dm**   **G**   **Am**

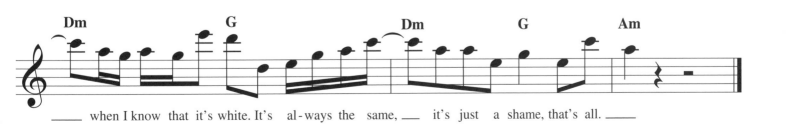

___ when I know that it's white. It's al - ways the same, ___ it's just a shame, that's all. _____

THIRTY DAYS IN THE HOLE

Words and Music by
STEVE MARRIOTT

Moderately

Chi - ca - go ___ Green, ___ talk - in' 'bout Black Leb - a - nese, ___

___ a dirt - y room ___ and a sil - ver coke ___ spoon ___

give me my re - lease. ___ Black Nap - a - lese, ___

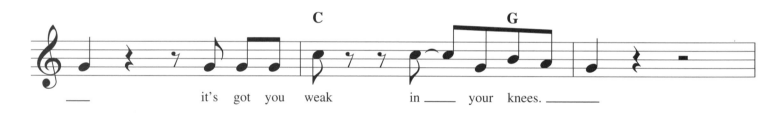

___ it's got you weak in ___ your knees. ___

Seize some dust ___ that you got bust ___ on; ___ you know it's hard to be - lieve. ___

Play 3 times

___ Thir - ty days in the hole, ___ thir - ty days in the

To Coda ⊕

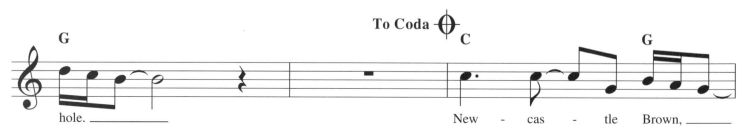

hole. ___ New - cas - tle Brown, ___

I'm tell - ing you, can sure smack __ you down. _____ Take a

greas - y whore __ and a roll - in' dance __ floor; _____

it's got your head spin - nin' 'round. _____ If you

live on __ the road, well, there's a new high - way code, _____

__ you take the ur - ban noise __ with some Dur - ban Poi - son, _____

D.S. al Coda
(with repeats)

it's gon - na less - en your load. _____ Thir - ty days in the

CODA

Black Nap - a - lese, _____ it's got you

TUSH

Words and Music by BILLY F GIBBONS,
DUSTY HILL and FRANK LEE BEARD

TIME FOR ME TO FLY

Words and Music by
KEVIN CRONIN

Moderately slow

I've been a-round _____ for you, been up and down ___
You said we'd work _____ it out. You said that you had ___

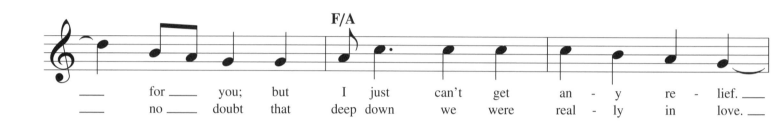

___ for _____ you; but I just can't get an-y re-lief. ___
___ no ___ doubt that deep down we were real-ly in love. ___

___ I've swal-lowed my pride ___
___ But I'm tired of hold -

___ for you, lived and lied _____ for _____ you; but
- ing on to a feel-ing I know _____ is _____ gone. I

you still make me feel like a thief. _____
do be-lieve me that I've had e-nough. _____

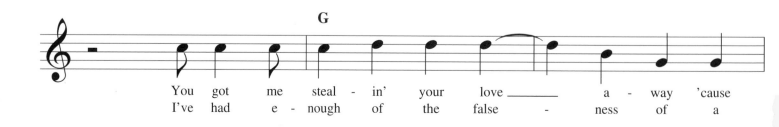

You got me steal-in' your love _____ a-way 'cause
I've had e-nough of the false-ness of a

you nev - er give _____ it;   peel - in' the years ___
worn - out re - la - tion;   e - nough of the jeal -

_____ a - way and we can't re - live _____ it.
- ous - y and the in - tol - er - a - tion.

I make you laugh, _____ and ___ you make me cry. ___

_____ I be - lieve it's time ___ for me ___ to fly. ___

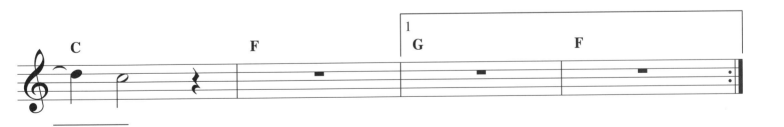

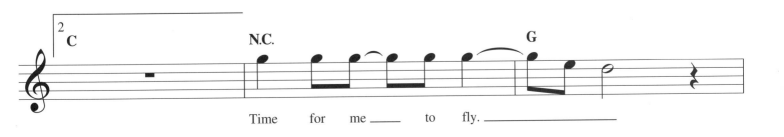

Time for me ___ to fly. _____

232

I've got to set _____ my - self free. Time for me ___ to fly. ___

_____ That's just how it's got to ___ be. ___

_____ I know it hurts to say ___ good -

bye, _____ but it's time for me ___ to fly. _____

_____ It's

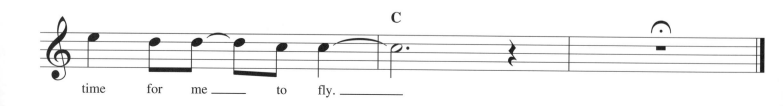

time for me ___ to fly. _____

WON'T GET FOOLED AGAIN

Words and Music by
PETER TOWNSHEND

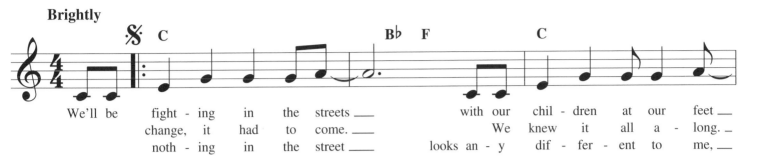

We'll be fight-ing in the streets ___ with our chil-dren at our feet ___
change, it had to come. ___ We knew it all a - long. ___
noth - ing in the street ___ looks an - y dif - fer - ent to me, ___

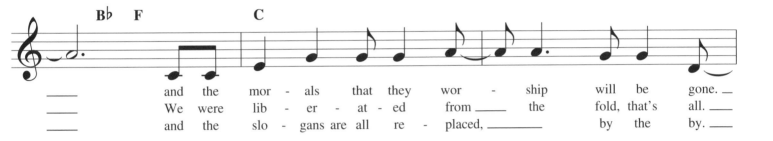

___ and the mor - als that they wor - ship will be gone. ___
___ We were lib - er - at - ed from ___ the fold, that's all. ___
___ and the slo - gans are all re - placed, ___ by the by. ___

___ And the men who spurred us on ___
___ The world looks just the same, ___
___ The part - ing on the left ___

___ sit in judg - ment of all wrong. ___ They de -
___ and his - to - ry ain't blamed, ___ 'cause the
___ is now a part - ing on the right, ___ and the

cide and a shot - gun sings the song. ___
ban - ners were all flown ___ in the last war. ___
beards have all grown long - er o - ver - night. ___

234

WALK THIS WAY

Words and Music by STEVEN TYLER
and JOE PERRY

Moderately fast, in 2

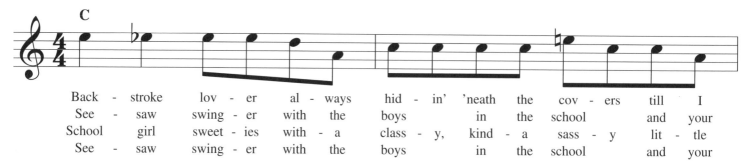

Back - stroke lov - er al - ways hid - in' 'neath the cov - ers till I
See - saw swing - er with the boys in the school and your
School girl sweet - ies with - a class - y, kind - a sass - y lit - tle
See - saw swing - er with the boys in the school and your

talked to your dad - dy, he say, _____ he said, "You
feet fly - in' up in the air, _____ sing - in',
skirts climb - in' way up their knees; _____ there was
feet fly - in' up in the air, _____ sing - in',

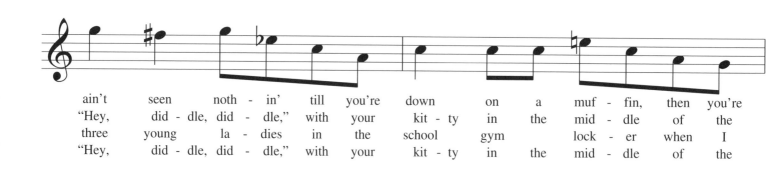

ain't seen noth - in' till you're down on a muf - fin, then you're
"Hey, did - dle, did - dle," with your kit - ty in the mid - dle of the
three young la - dies in the school gym lock - er when I
"Hey, did - dle, did - dle," with your kit - ty in the mid - dle of the

sure to be a - chang - in' your ways." _____ I met a
swing like you did - n't care. _____ So I
no - ticed they was look - in' at me. _____ I was a
swing like you did - n't care. _____ So I

cheer - lead - er, was a real young bleed - er, oh, the
took a big____ chance at the real high school dance with a
high school los - er, nev - er made it with a la - dy till the
took a big____ chance at the high school dance with a

times I could rem - i - nisce;____ 'cause the
miss - y who was read - y to play.____ Was - n't
boys told me some - thin' I missed.____ Then my
miss - y who was read - y to play.____ Was - n't

best things of lov - in' with her sis - ter and her cous - in on - ly
me she was fool - in' 'cause she knew what she was do - in' when I
next - door neigh - bor with a daugh - ter had a fa - vor, so I
me she was fool - in' 'cause she knew what she was do - in' when she

1, 3

start - ed with a lit - tle kiss____ like this.
knowed love was here to stay __ ____ when she told me to
gave her just a lit - tle kiss____ like this.
taught me how to walk this way. __ ____ She told me to

2, 4

C

walk this __ way, ____

F7

talk this __ way, ____

1–3

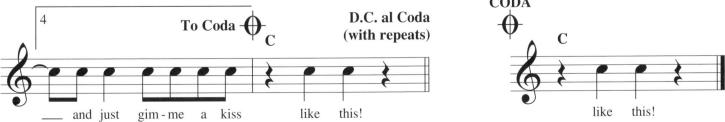

4 **To Coda ⊕** **C** **D.C. al Coda** **CODA ⊕**
(with repeats) **C**

____ and just gim - me a kiss like this! like this!

WE ARE THE CHAMPIONS

Words and Music by
FREDDIE MERCURY

Moderately slow

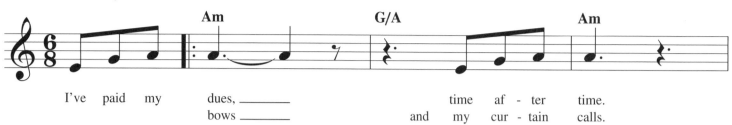

I've paid my dues, _____ time af - ter time.
bows _____ and my cur - tain calls.

I've done my _____ sen - tence but com - mit - ted no _____
You brought me fame and fortune and ev - 'ry-thing that goes with it, I thank you

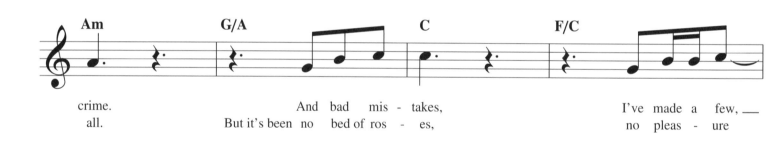

crime. And bad mis - takes, I've made a few, ___
all. But it's been no bed of ros - es, no pleas - ure

_____ I've had my share of sand ___ kicked in my ___
cruise. _____ I con - sid -er it a chal - lenge be - fore the whole hu - man

face but I've come through. ⎫ And I need to go on, and on, and
race and I ain't gon - na lose. ⎭

WE WILL ROCK YOU

Words and Music by
BRIAN MAY

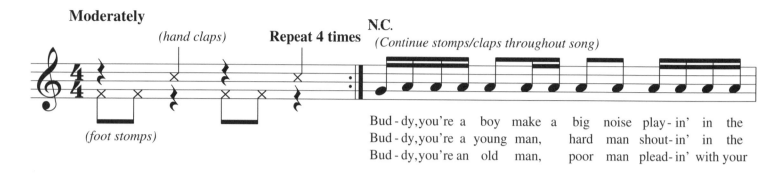

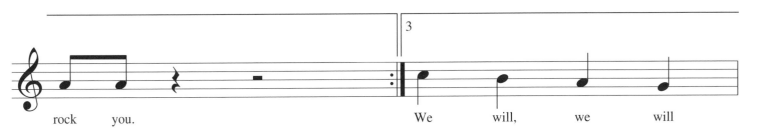

rock   you.   We   will,   we   will

rock   you.   We   will,   we   will   rock   you.

We   will,   we   will   rock   you.   *(Instrumental)*

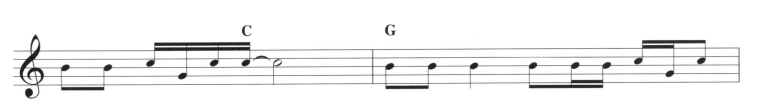

Repeat 3 times

WHEEL IN THE SKY

Words and Music by ROBERT FLEISCHMAN,
NEAL SCHON and DIANE VALORY

Moderate Rock

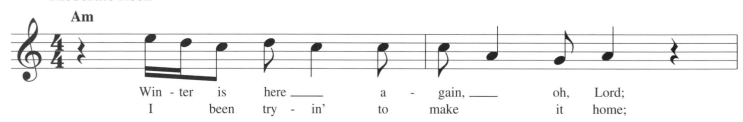

Win - ter is here ____ a - gain, ____ oh, Lord;
I been try - in' to make it home;

have - n't been home ____ in a year or _____ more. ____
got to make it be - fore too long. _____

I hope she holds ____ on ____ a lit - tle long - er. ____
Ooo, I can't take this ver - y much long - er. ____

(Instrumental)

Sent a let - ter on a
I'm stand - in' in the

long sum - mer day made ____ of sil - ver, not of clay. _____
sleet and rain. Don't think I'm nev - er gon - na make it home a - gain. _____

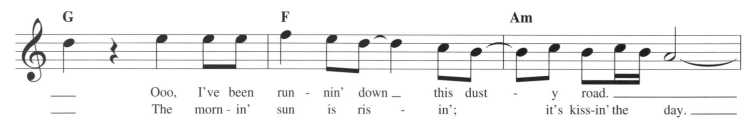

____ Ooo, I've been run - nin' down ____ this dust - y road. _____
____ The morn - in' sun is ris - in'; it's kiss-in' the day. ____

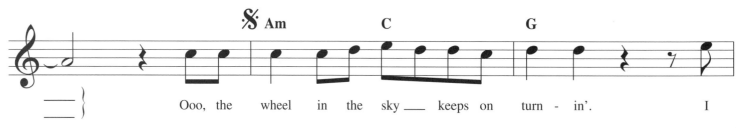

____ Ooo, the wheel in the sky ____ keeps on turn - in'. I

Am C   G   Am   C

don't know where I'll be to - mor - row. ___ {(1., 2.) Wheel in the sky __ keeps on
             (3.) Wheel in the sky __ keeps me

G   D/F♯ G   Dm/F   To Coda ⊕

turn - in'. }
yearn - in'. }   Whoa. _____

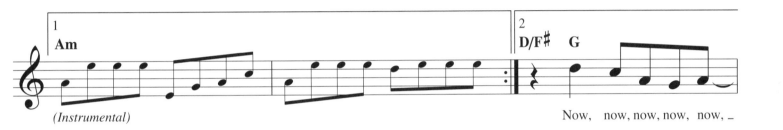

1
Am   2
                 D/F♯ G

(Instrumental)   Now, now, now, now, now, _

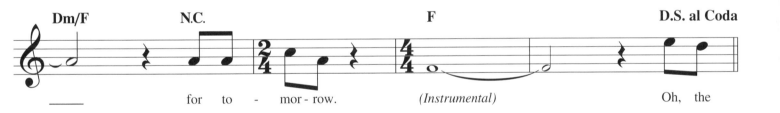

Dm/F   N.C.   F   D.S. al Coda

____   for to - mor - row.   *(Instrumental)*   Oh, the

CODA ⊕

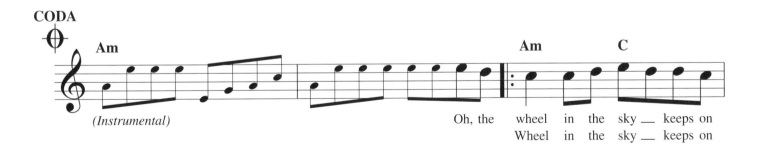

Am   Am   C

(Instrumental)   Oh, the wheel in the sky __ keeps on
                Wheel in the sky __ keeps on

G   Am   C   G   Am

turn - in'.   I don't know where I'll be to - mor - row. __
turn - in'.   I don't know, I don't know, I don't know. ___

A WHITER SHADE OF PALE

Words and Music by KEITH REID,
GARY BROOKER and MATTHEW FISHER

In a slow 4

We skipped the light ___ fan - dan - go, _____
She said, "I'm home ___ on shore leave," _____
She said, "There is ___ no rea - son, _____

turned cart - wheels ___ 'cross the floor. ___
though in truth we ___ were at sea. ___
and the truth is ___ plain to see." ___

I was feel - ing kind of sea - sick;
So I took her by the looking glass
But I wan - dered through my play-ing cards

the crowd called ___ out _____ for more.
and forced her ___ to _____ a - gree,
and would not ___ let _____ her be

YOU AIN'T SEEN NOTHIN' YET

Words and Music by
RANDY BACHMAN

Moderate Rock

I met a dev - il wom - an,   she
now I'm feel - in' bet - ter   'cause

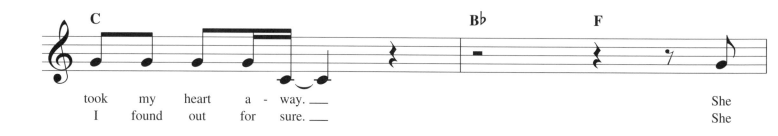

took my heart a - way. ___   She
I found out for sure. ___   She

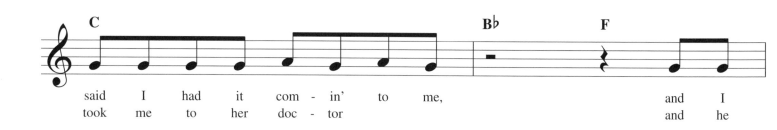

said I had it com - in' to me,   and I
took me to her doc - tor   and he

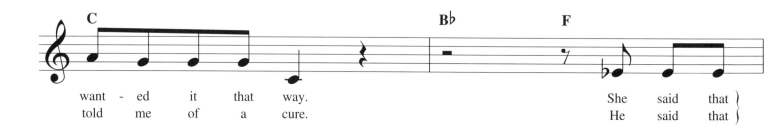

want - ed it that way.   She said that
told me of a cure.   He said that

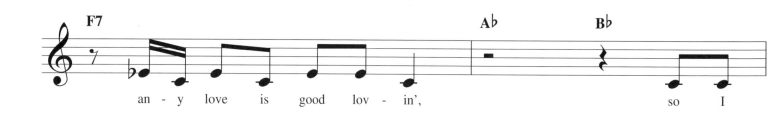

an - y love is good lov - in',   so I

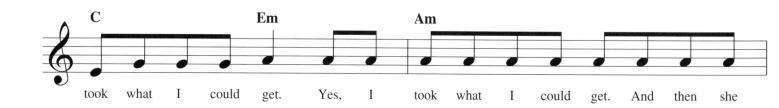

took what I could get. Yes, I took what I could get. And then she

looked at me ____ with those big brown eyes and she said: ____ "You

ain't seen noth - in' yet. B - b - b - ba - by, you just

ain't seen noth - in' yet. Here's some - thin', here's some - thin', here's

some - thin' you ain't nev - er gon - na for - get, ba - by.

Ya know, ____ ya know, ya know, ya know you just

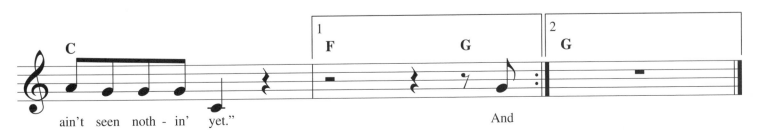

ain't seen noth - in' yet." And

YOU MAKE LOVIN' FUN

Words and Music by
CHRISTINE McVIE

Moderate Rock beat

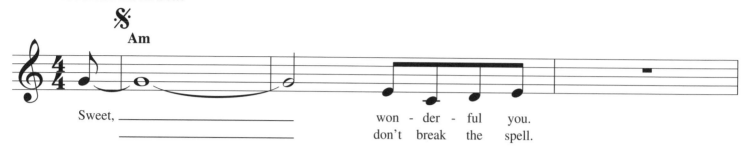

Sweet, _____ _____ won - der - ful you.
_____ don't break the spell.

You make me hap - py with the things you do. _____
It would be dif - f'rent, and you know it will. _____

— Oh, _____
— You, _____

— can it be so?
— you make lov - ing fun.

This feel - ing fol - lows me wher - ev - er I go. _____
And I don't have _____ to tell you you're the on - ly _____

YOU REALLY GOT ME

Words and Music by
RAY DAVIES

Working for the Weekend

Words and Music by PAUL DEAN,
MATTHEW FRENETTE and MICHAEL RENO

Moderate Rock

Ev - 'ry-one's watch - in' to
Ev - 'ry-one's look - in' to

see what you will do. _____ Ev - 'ry-one's look -
see if it was you. _____ Ev - 'ry-one wants _____

- in' at you, _____ ooh. _____
_____ you to come through. _____

Ev - 'ry-one's won - der - in' will you come out to - night. _____
Ev - 'ry-one's hop - in' _____ it - 'll _____ all work out. _____

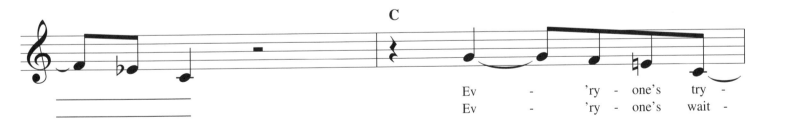

_____ Ev - 'ry - one's try -
_____ Ev - 'ry - one's wait -

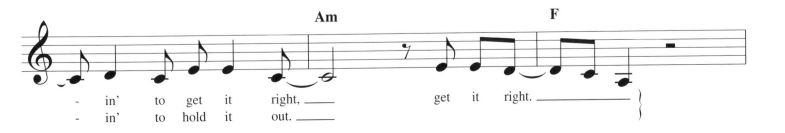

- in' to get it right, _____ get it right. _____
- in' to hold it out. _____

Ev - 'ry - bod - y's work - in' for ___ the week - end.

Ev - 'ry - bod - y wants ___ a new ___ ro - mance.

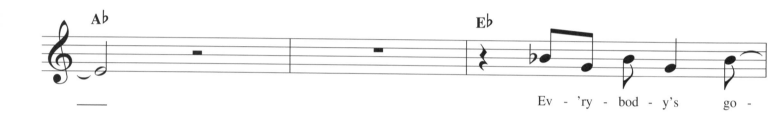

___ Ev - 'ry - bod - y's go -

- in' off ___ the deep ___ end.

Ev - 'ry - bod - y needs ___ a sec - ond chance, ___ oh. ___

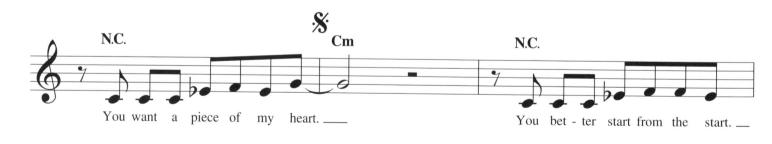

You want a piece of my heart. ___ You bet - ter start from the start. ___

___ You wan - na be in the show. ___

CHORD SPELLER

C chords

C	C–E–G
Cm	C–E♭–G
C7	C–E–G–B♭
Cdim	C–E♭–G♭
C+	C–E–G♯

C♯ or D♭ chords

C♯	C♯–F–G♯
C♯m	C♯–E–G♯
C♯7	C♯–F– G♯–B
C♯dim	C♯–E–G
C♯+	C♯–F–A

D chords

D	D–F♯–A
Dm	D–F–A
D7	D–F♯–A–C
Ddim	D–F–A♭
D+	D–F♯–A♯

E♭ chords

E♭	E♭–G–B♭
E♭m	E♭–G♭–B♭
E♭7	E♭–G–B♭–D♭
E♭dim	E♭–G♭–A
E♭+	E♭–G–B

E chords

E	E–G♯–B
Em	E–G–B
E7	E–G♯–B–D
Edim	E–G–B♭
E+	E–G♯–C

F chords

F	F–A–C
Fm	F–A♭–C
F7	F–A–C–E♭
Fdim	F–A♭–B
F+	F–A–C♯

F♯ or G♭ chords

F♯	F♯–A♯–C♯
F♯m	F♯–A–C♯
F♯7	F♯–A♯–C♯–E
F♯dim	F♯–A–C
F♯+	F♯–A♯–D

G chords

G	G–B–D
Gm	G–B♭–D
G7	G–B–D–F
Gdim	G–B♭–D♭
G+	G–B–D♯

G♯ or A♭ chords

A♭	A♭–C–E♭
A♭m	A♭–B–E♭
A♭7	A♭–C–E♭–G♭
A♭dim	A♭–B–D
A♭+	A♭–C–E

A chords

A	A–C♯–E
Am	A–C–E
A7	A–C♯–E–G
Adim	A–C–E♭
A+	A–C♯–F

B♭ chords

B♭	B♭–D–F
B♭m	B♭–D♭–F
B♭7	B♭–D–F–A♭
B♭dim	B♭–D♭–E
B♭+	B♭–D–F♯

B chords

B	B–D♯–F♯
Bm	B–D–F♯
B7	B–D♯–F♯–A
Bdim	B–D–F
B+	B–D♯–G

Important Note: A slash chord (C/E, G/B) tells you that a certain bass note is to be played under a particular harmony. In the case of C/E, the chord is C and the bass note is E.

HAL LEONARD PRESENTS
FAKE BOOKS FOR BEGINNERS!

Entry-level fake books! These books feature larger-than-most fake book notation with simplified harmonies and melodies – and all songs are in the key of C. An introduction addresses basic instruction in playing from a fake book.

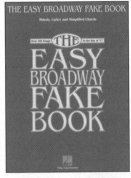

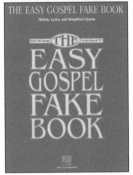

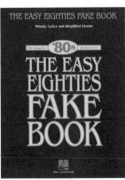

YOUR FIRST FAKE BOOK
00240112...$19.95

THE EASY FAKE BOOK
00240144...$19.95

THE SIMPLIFIED FAKE BOOK
00240168...$19.95

THE BEATLES EASY FAKE BOOK
00240309...$25.00

THE EASY BROADWAY FAKE BOOK
00240180...$19.95

THE EASY CHRISTMAS FAKE BOOK – 2ND EDITION
00240209...$19.95

THE EASY CLASSICAL FAKE BOOK
00240262...$19.95

THE EASY CHRISTIAN FAKE BOOK
00240328...$19.99

THE EASY COUNTRY FAKE BOOK
00240319...$19.95

THE EASY EARLY SONGS FAKE BOOK
00240337 ....$19.99

THE EASY FOLKSONG FAKE BOOK
00240360...$19.99

THE EASY GOSPEL FAKE BOOK
00240169...$19.95

THE EASY HYMN FAKE BOOK
00240207...$19.95

THE EASY LATIN FAKE BOOK
00240333...$19.99

THE EASY MOVIE FAKE BOOK
00240295...$19.95

THE EASY SHOW TUNES FAKE BOOK
00240297...$19.95

THE EASY STANDARDS FAKE BOOK
00240294...$19.95

THE EASY WORSHIP FAKE BOOK
00240265...$19.95

THE EASY TWENTIES FAKE BOOK
00240336 ....$19.99

THE EASY THIRTIES FAKE BOOK
00240335 ....$19.99

THE EASY FORTIES FAKE BOOK
00240252...$19.95

MORE OF THE EASY FORTIES FAKE BOOK
00240287...$19.95

THE EASY FIFTIES FAKE BOOK
00240255...$19.95

MORE OF THE EASY FIFTIES FAKE BOOK
00240288...$19.95

THE EASY SIXTIES FAKE BOOK
00240253...$19.95

MORE OF THE EASY SIXTIES FAKE BOOK
00240289...$19.95

THE EASY SEVENTIES FAKE BOOK
00240256...$19.95

MORE OF THE EASY SEVENTIES FAKE BOOK
00240290...$19.95

THE EASY EIGHTIES FAKE BOOK
00240340 ....$19.99

THE EASY NINETIES FAKE BOOK
00240341 ....$19.99

FOR MORE INFORMATION,
SEE YOUR LOCAL MUSIC DEALER,
OR WRITE TO:

HAL•LEONARD®
CORPORATION
7777 W. BLUEMOUND RD. P.O. BOX 13819
MILWAUKEE, WISCONSIN 53213

www.halleonard.com

Prices, contents and availability subject to change without notice.

0711

THE ULTIMATE COLLECTION OF
FAKE BOOKS

The Real Book – Sixth Edition

Hal Leonard proudly presents the first legitimate and legal editions of these books ever produced. These bestselling titles are mandatory for anyone who plays jazz! Over 400 songs, including: All By Myself • Dream a Little Dream of Me • God Bless the Child • Like Someone in Love • When I Fall in Love • and more.

00240221	Volume 1, C Edition	$32.50
00240224	Volume 1, B♭ Edition	$32.50
00240225	Volume 1, E♭ Edition	$32.50
00240226	Volume 1, BC Edition	$32.50
00240222	Volume 2, C Edition	$29.99
00240227	Volume 2, B♭ Edition	$29.95
00240228	Volume 2, E♭ Edition	$32.50

Best Fake Book Ever – 3rd Edition

More than 1,000 songs from all styles of music, including: All My Loving • At the Hop • Cabaret • Dust in the Wind • Fever • From a Distance • Hello, Dolly! • Hey Jude • King of the Road • Longer • Misty • Route 66 • Sentimental Journey • Somebody • Song Sung Blue • Spinning Wheel • Unchained Melody • We Will Rock You • What a Wonderful World • Wooly Bully • Y.M.C.A. • and more.

00290239	C Edition	$49.99
00240083	B♭ Edition	$49.95
00240084	E♭ Edition	$49.95

Classic Rock Fake Book – 2nd Edition

This fake book is a great compilation of more than 250 terrific songs of the rock era, arranged for piano, voice, guitar and all C instruments. Includes: All Right Now • American Woman • Birthday • Honesty • I Shot the Sheriff • I Want You to Want Me • Imagine • It's Still Rock and Roll to Me • Lay Down Sally • Layla • My Generation • Rock and Roll All Nite • Spinning Wheel • White Room • We Will Rock You • lots more!

00240108 .... $29.95

Classical Fake Book – 2nd Edition

This unprecedented, amazingly comprehensive reference includes over 850 classical themes and melodies for all classical music lovers. Includes everything from Renaissance music to Vivaldi and Mozart to Mendelssohn. Lyrics in the original language are included when appropriate.

00240044 .... $34.95

The Disney Fake Book – 3rd Edition

Over 200 of the most beloved songs of all time, including: Be Our Guest • Can You Feel the Love Tonight • Colors of the Wind • Cruella De Vil • Friend Like Me • Heigh-Ho • It's a Small World • Mickey Mouse March • Supercalifragilisticexpialidocious • Under the Sea • When You Wish upon a Star • A Whole New World • Zip-A-Dee-Doo-Dah • and more!

00240039 .... $27.99

The Folksong Fake Book

Over 1,000 folksongs perfect for performers, school teachers, and hobbyists. Includes: Bury Me Not on the Lone Prairie • Clementine • Danny Boy • The Erie Canal • Go, Tell It on the Mountain • Home on the Range • Kumbaya • Michael Row the Boat Ashore • Shenandoah • Simple Gifts • Swing Low, Sweet Chariot • When Johnny Comes Marching Home • Yankee Doodle • and many more.

00240151 .... $24.95

The Hymn Fake Book

Nearly 1,000 multi-denominational hymns perfect for church musicians or hobbyists: Amazing Grace • Christ the Lord Is Risen Today • For the Beauty of the Earth • It Is Well with My Soul • A Mighty Fortress Is Our God • O for a Thousand Tongues to Sing • Praise to the Lord, the Almighty • Take My Life and Let It Be • What a Friend We Have in Jesus • and hundreds more!

00240145 .... $24.95

The Praise & Worship Fake Book

400 songs: As the Deer • Better Is One Day • Come, Now Is the Time to Worship • Firm Foundation • Glorify Thy Name • Here I Am to Worship • I Could Sing of Your Love Forever • Lord, I Lift Your Name on High • More Precious Than Silver • Open the Eyes of My Heart • The Power of Your Love • Shine, Jesus, Shine • Trading My Sorrows • We Fall Down • You Are My All in All • and more.

00240234 .... $34.95

The R&B Fake Book – 2nd Edition

This terrific fake book features 375 classic R&B hits: Baby Love • Best of My Love • Dancing in the Street • Easy • Get Ready • Heatwave • Here and Now • Just Once • Let's Get It On • The Loco-Motion • (You Make Me Feel Like) A Natural Woman • One Sweet Day • Papa Was a Rollin' Stone • Save the Best for Last • September • Sexual Healing • Shop Around • Still • Tell It Like It Is • Up on the Roof • Walk on By • What's Going On • more!

00240107 C Edition $29.95

Ultimate Broadway Fake Book – 5th Edition

More than 700 show-stoppers from over 200 shows! Includes: Ain't Misbehavin' • All I Ask of You • Bewitched • Camelot • Don't Cry for Me Argentina • Edelweiss • I Dreamed a Dream • If I Were a Rich Man • Memory • Oklahoma • Send in the Clowns • What I Did for Love • more.

00240046 .... $49.99

FOR MORE INFORMATION, SEE YOUR LOCAL MUSIC DEALER, OR WRITE TO:

HAL•LEONARD® CORPORATION

7777 W. BLUEMOUND RD. P.O. BOX 13819 MILWAUKEE, WI 53213

Complete songlists available online at www. halleonard.com

The Ultimate Christmas Fake Book – 5th Edition

This updated edition includes 275 traditional and contemporary Christmas songs: Away in a Manger • The Christmas Song • Deck the Hall • Frosty the Snow Man • A Holly Jolly Christmas • I Heard the Bells on Christmas Day • Jingle Bells • Little Saint Nick • Merry Christmas, Darling • Nuttin' for Christmas • Rudolph the Red-Nosed Reindeer • Silent Night • What Child Is This? • more.

00240045 .... $24.95

The Ultimate Country Fake Book – 5th Edition

This book includes over 700 of your favorite country hits: Always on My Mind • Boot Scootin' Boogie • Crazy • Down at the Twist and Shout • Forever and Ever, Amen • Friends in Low Places • The Gambler • Jambalaya • King of the Road • Sixteen Tons • There's a Tear in My Beer • Your Cheatin' Heart • and hundreds more.

00240049 .... $49.99

The Ultimate Fake Book – 4th Edition

Includes over 1,200 hits: Blue Skies • Body and Soul • Endless Love • A Foggy Day • Isn't It Romantic? • Memory • Mona Lisa • Moon River • Operator • Piano Man • Roxanne • Satin Doll • Shout • Small World • Speak Softly, Love • Strawberry Fields Forever • Tears in Heaven • Unforgettable • hundreds more!

00240024	C Edition	$49.95
00240026	B♭ Edition	$49.95
00240025	E♭ Edition	$49.95

The Ultimate Pop/Rock Fake Book – 4th Edition

Over 600 pop standards and contemporary hits, including: All Shook Up • Another One Bites the Dust • Crying • Don't Know Much • Dust in the Wind • Earth Angel • Every Breath You Take • Hero • Hey Jude • Hold My Hand • Imagine • Layla • The Loco-Motion • Oh, Pretty Woman • On Broadway • Spinning Wheel • Stand by Me • Stayin' Alive • Tears in Heaven • True Colors • The Twist • Vision of Love • A Whole New World • Wild Thing • Wooly Bully • Yesterday • more!

00240099 .... $39.99

Fake Book of the World's Favorite Songs – 4th Edition

Over 700 favorites, including: America the Beautiful • Anchors Aweigh • Battle Hymn of the Republic • Bill Bailey, Won't You Please Come Home • Chopsticks • Für Elise • His Eye Is on the Sparrow • I Wonder Who's Kissing Her Now • Jesu, Joy of Man's Desiring • My Old Kentucky Home • Sidewalks of New York • Take Me Out to the Ball Game • When the Saints Go Marching In • and hundreds more!

00240072 .... $22.95